A 14-DAY
Romance Challenge

SHARON JAYNES

HARVEST HOUSE PUBLISHERS
EUGENE, OREGON

Unless otherwise indicated, all Scripture quotations are taken from the Holy Bible, New International Version®, NIV®. Copyright © 1973, 1978, 1984, 2011 by Biblica, Inc.® Used by permission. All rights reserved worldwide.

Verses marked NKJV are taken from the New King James Version®. Copyright © 1982 by Thomas Nelson, Inc. Used by permission. All rights reserved.

Verses marked NLT are taken from the *Holy Bible*, New Living Translation, copyright ©1996, 2004, 2007, 2013 by Tyndale House Foundation. Used by permission of Tyndale House Publishers, Inc., Carol Stream, Illinois 60188. All rights reserved.

Verses marked MSG are taken from THE MESSAGE. Copyright © by Eugene H. Peterson 1993, 1994, 1995, 1996, 2000, 2001, 2002. Used by permission of Tyndale House Publishers, Inc.

Cover by www.DesignByJulia.com, Woodland Park, CO

Cover Images © Ruth Black / ShutterStock

A 14-DAY ROMANCE CHALLENGE

Copyright © 2017 Sharon Jaynes
Published by Harvest House Publishers
Eugene, Oregon 97402
www.harvesthousepublishers.com

ISBN 978-0-7369-6969-7 (pbk.)
ISBN 978-0-7369-6970-3 (eBook)

Library of Congress Cataloging-in-Publication Data
Names: Jaynes, Sharon, author.
Title: A 14-day romance challenge / Sharon Jaynes.
Other titles: Fourteen-day romance challenge
Description: Eugene, Oregon : Harvest House Publishers, 2017.
Identifiers: LCCN 2016037596 | ISBN 9780736969697 (pbk.)
Subjects: LCSH: Marriage—Religious aspects—Christianity. | Sex in marriage.
  | Sex in marriage—Religious aspects—Christianity. | Wives. |
  Men—Psychology.
Classification: LCC BV835 .J39 2017 | DDC 248.8/435—dc23 LC record available at https://lccn.loc.gov/2016037596

All rights reserved. No part of this publication may be reproduced, stored in a retrieval system, or transmitted in any form or by any means—electronic, mechanical, digital, photocopy, recording, or any other—except for brief quotations in printed reviews, without the prior permission of the publisher.

Printed in the United States of America

17 18 19 20 21 22 23 24 / BP-SK / 10 9 8 7 6 5 4 3 2

Contents

Welcome to the 14-Day Romance Challenge!

Have you ever wondered what your husband longs for in the woman of his dreams? Chances are he won't tell you, but he told me. Well, maybe not *your* husband, but hundreds of men just like him did. And he wants a little romance.

I remember my wedding day. I bet you remember yours too. Before I walked into that sanctuary, I looked in the mirror in the bride's room and thought about all the women who had walked the aisle before me—women so full of promise and hope. I pondered what could possibly go wrong that so many marriages end in divorce. Over the years—36 of them at the time of this writing—I have discovered the answer to that question. A lot can go wrong.

I don't have a big, bad personal story of how God took a terrible, tumultuous marriage and miraculously transformed it into a storybook romance filled with white-knight rescues, relentless romance, and rides into the sunset leaving all danger and darkness behind. Although our marriage has been all that at one time or another, it's no fairy tale.

Our marriage is a daily journal, one page after another, one day after another. Some entries are smudged with tears; others are dog-eared as favorites. Some days are marred by unsuccessful erasures that couldn't quite rub away the words said; others are finger-worn by the reading of precious events time and time again.

One of the dangers of a good marriage is that we can take it for granted. We get up in the morning, make breakfast, go to work, run errands, come home, eat dinner, deal with kids, watch TV, go to bed, and get up the next day to do it all over again. On the weekends we manage the bigger chores, go to kids' activities, watch more TV, go to church, and, well, you get the picture. Life falls into a rhythm and routine, and marriage can become mundane, lacking enthusiasm, excitement, and zeal.

None of us got married so we could have a long list of chores. Most likely you got married because you were madly in love and couldn't imagine life without your man! You got married because you were passionately, sexually, and romantically stirred beyond belief. You couldn't wait to tie the knot and crawl into bed every night with this incredible person God had miraculously brought into your life. Maybe you still feel that way. But maybe you could use a little reminder—a re-stoking of that passion.

For most of us, life is just daily. However, the accumulation of small struggles can nibble like termites to undermine the foundation of what appears to be a healthy structure as surely as the unexpected, earth-shaking rumble of sudden disaster. And routine, even good routine, can rob us of the joy of marriage if we let it.

That's where the 14-Day Romance Challenge comes in. We're going to shake it up a bit! And spice it up a lot!

You are about to embark on an exciting journey of romancing your husband…and it's going to be fun! Before I wrote the book *Becoming the Woman of His Dreams: Seven Qualities Every Man Longs For,* I interviewed hundreds of men to find out what they longed for in a wife. The woman of a man's dreams

♥ **p** rays for him

♥ **r** espects him

♥ **a** dmires him

♥ **i** nitiates intimate friendship

♥ **s** afeguards their marriage

♥ **e** ncourages him

♥ **s** exually fulfills him

The first letter from each of those words spells PRAISES, which points to the words of a husband praising his wife in the book of Proverbs: "Her husband…praises her, 'Many women do noble things, but you surpass them all'" (Proverbs 31:28-29).

But in this 14-day challenge, we're focusing on just *one* aspect of what your man longs for. Snuggled into his desire to be admired is his secret longing to be romanced. Yes, your husband longs to be romanced by the woman of his dreams.

Each day you'll read a short capsule of encouragement and

a few snippets from *Becoming the Woman of His Dreams*. Then you'll review five Romance Challenge Ideas. Some of the challenges are simpler than others. Some are spicier than others. They range from mildly warm to hot and spicy. You get to pick the challenge that's right for you, depending on how high you want the flames to burn.

I've also included some responses from the men who completed my survey for *Becoming the Woman of His Dreams*. You'll see those in a section titled Here's What the Guys Said. I think you'll find their honest responses eye-opening, heart-tugging, and yes, challenging.

In addition, you'll see some responses from women who went through the challenge. I hope these will encourage you to keep moving forward and not give up!

If you're familiar with my blog at www.sharonjaynes.com, you know I love locking arms with other women. I hope you do too. So why not invite a few girlfriends to join you in the 14-Day Romance Challenge?

Here's a note you can copy and paste to invite your married friends, coworkers, or family members to join you. (Oh, the stories you will tell!)

> *Hi, friend! Could your marriage use a little spicing up in the romance department? If so, I'd like to invite you to join me in taking the 14-Day Romance Challenge with bestselling author Sharon Jaynes. Just click on www.romancechallenge.com and read more about the challenge, along with some comments from*

> *women who've given it a try. If you join me in the*
> *14-Day Romance Challenge, let me know! I'd love*
> *to compare notes and see the difference it made in*
> *your marriage.*

I'd love to pray for you as you take me up on this challenge to romance your husband. Send me an email at Sharon@sharonjaynes.com and let me know you've started. I'll begin praying for you as you honor God by loving your man well.

Be blessed!

Sharon

DAY 1

Romance—It's Not Just for Us Girls

If there's one thing I know about us girls, it's that we like romance! We love romance novels, romance comedies, romance tragedies, and romance, romance, romance. Most gals would much rather take in a romantic movie than an action film. And what woman doesn't dream about her husband romancing her the way he did when they were dating? But guess what, that man of yours longs for romance too.

One night Steve and I were planning a romantic evening at home alone. We borrowed a movie from our friends Gene and Sheri. *A Vow to Remember* promised to be a real tearjerker. The couple on the DVD case appeared lost in each other as their arms intertwined in a lovers' embrace. The back cover boasted, "Capture your mind, your heart and your soul...Paints a compelling picture of forever love."

The lights were dim, the candles were lit, and the mood was set. However, when Steve placed the movie in the DVD player, we were not greeted with strains of a melodious theme song or misty-eyed romance. Oh no. It was Arnold Schwarzenegger with machine gun at the ready! Our romantic evening was rudely interrupted by *Terminator*. Gene had placed the wrong movie in the case!

Perhaps romance in your marriage has a greater resemblance to *Terminator* than *A Vow to Remember*. If so, I'm so glad you've accepted the 14-Day Romance Challenge!

Willard Harley, author of *His Needs, Her Needs: Building an Affair-Proof Marriage*, notes that one way to affair-proof a marriage is for a husband and wife to become aware of each other's needs and learn to meet them.[1] On the surface, that seems obvious, but in reality, most couples don't realize what each other's needs truly are.

Harley lists the woman's five basic needs in marriage as:

1. Affection

2. Conversation

3. Honesty and Openness

4. Financial Support

5. Family Commitment

He lists the man's five basic needs in marriage as:

1. Sexual Fulfillment

2. Recreational Companionship

3. An Attractive Spouse

4. Domestic Support

5. Admiration[2]

When a wife doesn't feel cherished, she's not as
interested in having sex with her husband. When
a husband doesn't have sex, he doesn't feel like
showing affection to his wife. Okay. So that's a problem.
Someone has to make the first move. It could be you.

So for us gals, affection is paramount. For the guys, sex is key. How do we reconcile the two? Harley explains:

> When it comes to sex and affection, you can't have one without the other.[3]

> The typical wife doesn't understand her husband's deep need for sex any more than the typical husband understands his wife's deep need for affection.[4]

Harley notes that most men will tell you that they wish their wives were more sexual, and most women would say that they wish their husbands were more affectionate and romantic. Many men feel sexually cheated by their wives and many women feel emotionally cheated by their husbands.

When a wife doesn't feel cherished, she's not as interested in having sex with her husband. When a husband doesn't have sex, he doesn't feel like showing affection to his wife. Okay. So that's a problem. Someone has to make the first move. It could be you.

Jesus said, "So in everything, do to others what you would have them do to you," (Matthew 7:12). We call that the

Golden Rule. Isn't it interesting that a wedding ring is often called a band of gold? Whether a wedding ring is gold, platinum, silver, or bronze, the Golden Rule certainly applies in a marriage relationship.

We should never *give* with the ulterior motive of *receiving*. James warns that even our prayers can go unanswered when we pray with wrong motives (James 4:3). But the truth is, most of the time when we romance our husbands they become more romantic in return. The Golden Rule for romance could be, *Express your love to your husband in the same way you want him to express his love to you.* Sticky notes of love on his bathroom mirror, romantic texts in the middle of the day, and declarations of how proud you are of him are actually showing him ways to love you in return.

When a wife ignores her man's sexual needs, it's a slap in the face that says, "I don't care about you or our marriage." Some might say, "Well, the same goes for him! If he doesn't show me more affection, I'm not going to feel like having more sex! It's his fault we're in this mess!"

But friend, this little book isn't about what he needs to do. It's about what you can do. It's about how to minister to your husband. Is that an odd way to think about it? Is that a new thought for you?

Consider this: God fashioned your husband to be a sexual, visual, tactile human being. When you meet his needs, you are ministering to him in a way only you can. God planned it that way.

*We need to erase the line separating the sexual
and the sacred and realize that being intimate with
our husband is an opportunity to glorify God.*

In my book *A Sudden Glory: God's Lavish Response to Your Ache for Something More*, I wrote about how we tend to separate our spiritual lives and our secular lives. But the Bible never separates the two. As we live and move and have our being in Christ (Acts 17:28), all of life becomes an act of worship. Doing laundry to the glory of God. Singing praises to the glory of God. Frying bacon to the glory of God. Reading our Bibles to the glory of God.

We need to erase the line separating the secular and the sacred and realize that all of life is an opportunity to glorify God. Let me go one step further: we need to erase the line separating the sexual and the sacred and realize that even being intimate with our husband is an opportunity to glorify God. When you love your husband well, you are glorifying God in one of the most wonderful ways imaginable.

We all have needs, but God never intended for any human relationship to meet all those needs. Only God can do that. However, when it comes to romance, God has placed you as the sole proprietor of fulfilling that need in your man's life. And isn't that the way you want it to be? A wife doesn't want her man looking at any address other than hers for that particular need to be met…and exceedingly so.

Going back to Harley's five needs for every man and five

needs for every woman in marriage, where does romance fit in? Obviously it fits in with the woman's need for affection and the man's need for sexual fulfillment. Not so obviously, romance touches on each of the other four needs of your man as well.

♥ Romance is stirred by recreational companionship—having fun together creates romantic ties and lasting memories. It stirs up endorphins and a sense of well-being.

♥ Romance is stoked when a wife takes interest in her appearance for the purpose of wooing her man—he is attracted to her, and he is proud to call her his.

♥ Romance is stimulated when a wife takes steps to create a warm, orderly environment. He enjoys being home and appreciates the way his wife provides a place to rest, rejuvenate, and recreate.

♥ Romance is stepped up when a wife admires her husband. Oh my, there's nothing more romantic to a man than feeling that his wife admires him, is proud of him, and thinks he's the most amazing man on earth.

When we think of the romantic things, we think of events that occur because someone made a choice to love.

Many people believe affairs are birthed from unmet needs. And while that subject is beyond the scope of the 14-Day Romance Challenge, let me assure you that when you make time to keep your marriage a priority, you are not only taking steps to keep it strong; you are taking steps to affair-proof your marriage.

If you're a little anxious about how your husband will respond to your efforts, consider a few responses from women who have already completed the challenge:

> Thank you so much for this challenge. It was what I needed in more ways than one. I realized by doing just the little things how excited I was to do them and how excited my husband was to receive them. After the first two days, he asked me what was going on, and I told him to enjoy the next twelve! I told him I was doing this for him and did not expect anything in return. Ended up I received flowers, notes, and more hugs and kisses! This has been a HUGE spark to our 28-year marriage! It was fun to plan what to do each day and sneak around hiding things, putting notes in his car, and hiding something very fun in his gym bag! I shared this with some other girls, and they started doing the same thing! I even shared this with my daughter, and she did it for her husband.

And don't be surprised if you see some changes in your own heart. Here's what another woman, who had also been married 28 years, said about an unexpected result of the challenge:

> I feel I benefited just as much if not more from the challenge than my husband. We have been married 28 years and are still very much in love. But things can become routine. It did my heart and soul good to see my husband so happy with me. His usual reaction was a huge smile and a question: "What did I do to deserve this?"

In his book *The Romance Factor,* Alan Loy McGinnis notes,

> Being an artist at romance does not require so much a sentimental and emotional nature as it requires a thoughtful nature. When we think of the romantic things, we think of events that occur because someone made a choice to love. A man stops off at a florist and brings his wife a single rose in the evening, a girl makes her lover a lemon pie with just the degree of tartness he likes, a wife makes arrangements for her husband to take the caribou-hunting trip he thought he'd never afford—these are not the goo of sweet emotion. They are the stuff that comes from resolution and determination, and they are strong mortar."[5]

So let's get started with that strong mortar!

Romance Challenge Ideas

♥ Put a chocolate kiss in his briefcase, lunch bag, or on the dashboard of his car, with a note that says, "I love you!"

♥ Write "I love you" on his bathroom mirror with soap or lipstick.

♥ Send him a romantic card to his workplace via snail mail.

♥ Kiss him passionately before he leaves in the morning and tell him you're going to miss him. Kiss him passionately when he comes home in the evening and tell him you're glad he's home.

♥ Draw a bath, light candles, and invite him to join you. Lather him up with soap and draw a big heart on his chest. Lie in each other's arms and soak in the love.

Here's What the Guys Said

I wish my wife understood how important it is for a man to feel like he has made the mark. —Bart

The woman of my dreams is pretty (not beautiful). She has fun pampering me and is always affectionate. —Herman

The woman of my dreams understands how fragile a man's ego is. —Paul

I wish my wife understood how important being appreciated is. —Curt

Simple Surprises with Big Impact

It was a beautiful sunny day in Peoria, Illinois. Jill was so excited about the bouquet of surprises she had planned for her husband that she had slept very little the night before. As the first rays of sunshine peeped through the blinds, Jill quietly climbed out of bed and tiptoed into the kitchen. Moments later, she reappeared to awaken her prince with a kiss on his stubbly cheek and the aroma of waffles filling the room.

"Good morning, sunshine," she whispered. "Happy thirtieth birthday."

"What's this?" Jeremy mused.

"Breakfast in bed for the birthday boy."

Jeremy and Jill had been married for three years, and a recent move from Charlotte, North Carolina, to Peoria, Illinois, was a reminder that no matter what circumstances they faced in life, they moved as one. Jill had waited 31 years for the man of her dreams, and on this day, she was once again overwhelmed with the gift God had given her in Jeremy.

One of your husband's greatest longings is to be adored,
admired, and appreciated by the woman of his dreams.

After Jeremy finished his breakfast, Jill handed him a stack of note cards tied with red ribbon. The top card read "Jeremy Charles Tracey, here are 30 ways you are wonderful."

"Okay, now for your next surprise," Jill explained.

Jeremy gingerly removed the ribbon and began to read the cards.

"You are wonderful because you love the Lord."

"You are wonderful because you are handsome and sexy."

"You are wonderful because you are funny."

"You are wonderful because you are a great listener."

"You are wonderful because you make other people feel special."

"You are wonderful because you are talented and creative."

"You are wonderful because you are a great provider."

"You are wonderful because you are a wonderful son."

Through laughter and tears, Jeremy read each card aloud—one by one. Each card became a jewel in his birthday crown.

"I don't want to go to work today," Jeremy said as he hugged his bride. Little did he know the surprises that awaited him throughout the day. When he arrived at work, he found a list of 30 of their favorite memories. At lunch, his best friend appeared to take him to lunch.

What Jeremy had missed most after his move to Illinois was his best friend, prayer partner, and Sunday school teacher,

John Rinehart. Jill had arranged for John to fly to Peoria to share their special day. It was a tremendous surprise, and one Jeremy would never forget.

Jeremy's birthday was filled with surprises and acts of love, both big and small. At the end of the day, when Jill snuggled up beside her prince in bed, he held her tight and let the tears trickle down his face onto hers.

"I have never had even one surprise in all my birthdays. I still can't believe all you went through to make this day special." He then cupped her face in his hands and whispered, "You love me so much."

"You'd better believe I do," Jill said with a smile. "That's why I did all this. You are so special to me. I adore you."

> *Whether it is sharing a hot dog, or a myriad of simple surprises throughout the years romancing your husband will be creating a thousand strands of something unbreakable.*

One of your husband's greatest longings is to be adored, admired, and appreciated by the woman of his dreams. Too many times we walk down the aisle with a striking resemblance to Snow White but then somehow turn into the wicked queen. If that's the case in your home, fear not. The story is not over yet! You can draw a line in the sand and say, "No more." You can make a commitment to adore your husband and give him your best.

Bless him.
Edify him.
Share with him.
Touch him.

Whether it's sharing a hot dog at a baseball game or a myriad of simple surprises throughout the years, romancing your husband will be creating a thousand strands of what Sheldon Vanauken calls "something unbreakable." Consider his words about his relationship with his wife, Davy:

> "Look," we said, "what is it that draws two people into closeness and love? Of course there's the mystery of physical attraction, but beyond that it's the things they share. We both love strawberries and ships and collies and poems and all beauty, and all those things bind us together. Those sharings just happened to be; but what we must do now is share everything. If one of us likes anything, there must be something to like in it—and the other one must find it—every single thing that either of us likes. That way we shall create a thousand strands, great and small, that will link us together. Then we shall be so close that it would be impossible—unthinkable—for either of us to suppose that we could ever recreate such closeness with anyone else. And our trust in each other will not only be based on love and loyalty, but on the fact of a thousand sharings—a thousand strands twisted into something unbreakable."[1]

A simple surprise for your husband might be a night of intimacy he wasn't expecting. So as you carve out time for those simple surprises, don't forget to make time for the one thing that most says LOVE to him.

Now, let's take a look at how you can begin creating a strand of a thousand sharings and have your husband echo Jeremy's sentiment as he lays his head on the pillow at night: "You must really love me."

Here we go with Day 2 of the challenge!

Romance Challenge Ideas

♥ Make a list of 10 to 15 reasons you love your husband that begin with "You are wonderful because" or "I love you because." If you're really industrious, make a list of 50 reasons.

♥ Send him a text that says, "I'm thinking about you today."

♥ Warm up a towel in the dryer and greet him when he comes out of the shower in the morning. Wrap him with the towel and hand him a cup of steaming coffee.

♥ Put a note on his towel that says, "I envy this towel" and leave it hanging on its holder.

♥ Surprise him by joining him in the shower.

Here's What the Guys Said

I earn a good, six-figure income and work hard so my wife doesn't have to work outside the home, but I rarely feel appreciated. Instead, I feel like a nuisance because I might occasionally make a floor dirty or leave a cup out.
—Jim

The one thing that could make our marriage better is for my wife to appreciate and encourage me, but we've talked about that many times, and I'm afraid it's not going to change. —Jack

I wish my wife understood how hard I work for my family to provide for them. I long for more physical attention—hugs, hand-holding, sitting close. —Ben

DAY 3

The Golden Keys of Admiration and Appreciation

Where does your husband go for admiration and appreciation? He goes somewhere. All men do. Does he go to work in hopes of hearing "Job well done"? Does he go to the ball field in hopes of hearing "Way to go, man"? Does he go back home to mother to hear "I'm so proud of you, son"? Does he work late hoping for a few compliments from the gals in the office? Does he feast on compliments from patients or clients? Does he hang out at the gym flexing and building his biceps? Tell me, where does your man go to be admired?

> *Admiration and appreciation are the golden keys to unlocking a man's heart.*

In my first job as a dental hygienist, I noticed how the all-female staff, as well as the patients, admired the doctors in the building where I worked. I admired them too! They were a wonderful group of talented men who were gifted and skilled in their chosen profession. As a young woman in my early twenties, I wondered how the doctors' wives felt about the praise their hubbies received from other women all day long.

Amazingly, a few years later, I had the opportunity to find out for myself. After working for two years, I decided to go back to college. While there I met and married Steve Jaynes, a young dental student. When he started his practice, I remembered the admiring women from the years before, and I made a commitment that of all Steve's admirers he would have from the day he opened his practice until the day he retired, I was going to be his number one fan! And it wasn't long before I realized that admiration and appreciation are the golden keys to unlocking his heart.

Dr. Willard Harley says:

> When a woman tells a man she thinks he's wonderful, that inspires him to achieve more. He sees himself as capable of handling new responsibilities and perfecting skills far above those of his present level. That inspiration helps him prepare for the responsibilities of life. Admiration not only motivates, it also rewards the husband's existing achievements. When she tells him that she appreciates him for what he has done, it gives him more satisfaction than he receives from his paycheck. A woman needs to appreciate her husband for what he already is, not for what he could become, if he lived up to her standards. For some men—those with fragile self-images—admiration also helps them believe in themselves. Without it these men seem

> inherently more defensive about their shortcomings...While criticism causes men to become defensive, admiration energizes and motivates them. A man expects—and needs—his wife to be his most enthusiastic fan. He draws confidence from her support and can usually achieve far more with her.[1]

If you have been withholding admiring words from your husband, it may feel strange to begin. First and foremost, be authentic—be real. If you contrive admiring words, he'll be able to tell. Start with one compliment or one word of appreciation. It may be as simple as "thank you" and soon the admiration will begin to flow...hopefully both ways.

I'll admit that many of the ideas to romance your husband are what women would like. We love candlelit dinners, soft music, and love notes. That's not to say men don't like those things, but for them sex is key. God created them to be visually and tactilely (touch) stimulated. When talking to my husband about these ideas, he said, "The main reason guys will love these ideas is they show that their wives are thinking about them...and that means everything."

Dr. Harley explains the following about your husband's heart:

> Remember that a man really needs appreciation. He thrives on it. Many men who come to me because they have had affairs stress that the admiration of their lovers acted as a warm spring breeze in comparison to the arctic cold of their wives' criticism.

> How can they resist? Don't make your husband go
> outside your marriage for approval; he needs the
> perspective your appreciation gives him. That does
> not mean you have to fake it with him and tell him
> you love something that drives you wild, but work
> with him on the needs you must both fulfill, setting
> up a strategy that builds admiration.[2]

Not all men are admired at work. If work is a place where your husband meets opposition at every turn or leaves feeling like a failure, he will search for someplace to be admired. It may be on the softball field, on the racquetball court, as a deacon in the church, or through Facebook with old friends. How wonderful when that place is in your heart, in your arms, and in your home.

In his book *20 (Surprisingly Simple) Rules and Tools for a Great Marriage,* Dr. Steve Stephens lists four types of compliments: possession, appearance, behavior, and character.[3]

1. **Possession**, such as "I love that sweater on you."

2. **Appearance,** such as "That sweater brings out the blue in your eyes."

3. **Behavior**, such as "That was very sweet to let that driver go in front of you today."

4. **Character,** such as "Someone asked me what the definition of integrity was, and my mind immediately went to you." (I said that to my

husband, and he beamed from ear to ear. And I meant it.)

Look for ways to give your husband a compliment every day. Pay attention to him and take note of his appearance, behavior, and character qualities. Then sprinkle a few compliments his way. Your husband may be confused or skeptical with this sudden showering of praise. He may say, "What's up with the compliments all of a sudden?"

If that's his reaction, just say, "I'd forgotten what a wonderful man I'm married to, and I'm realizing it more and more every day!"

When you affirm your husband physically, emotionally, and verbally, you are blessing him in a way that no one else can.

Here's what one woman shared after showing her husband just how much she admired and appreciated him.

My husband and I have gone through the last 11 months dealing with infidelity on his part. As Christians, we have prayed for forgiveness for each other. It has been a struggle, but after being together 34 years, we just weren't ready to throw in the towel. The 14-Day Romance Challenge helped bring the spark back into our marriage, which is what was missing. It was instrumental in my husband seeking solace, admiration, and attention outside of our marriage…now he is getting that at home. We are growing stronger every day and I will continue to use your suggestions and show my husband that I love and cherish him, appreciate and adore him. And by the way, he has taken some of my ideas and showered them on me.

As a wife, you have great power to build up or tear down your husband. When you affirm your husband physically, emotionally, and verbally, you are blessing him in a way no one else can. Not only that, you are also glorifying God by honoring your marriage.

Here you are on Day 3! Maybe you haven't seen much of a reaction yet. Let me encourage you to keep going! Here's what one participant had to say:

I was tempted to give up on the third day but convicted to keep going. My husband's chest began to stick out each day after. He even shared with his coworkers what his wife was doing for him. By Day 14, he was past cloud nine.

So here we go with Day 3 of the Romance Challenge.

Romance Challenge Ideas

♥ Make a list of 10 to 15 reasons you appreciate or admire your husband and send it to him in an email, tape it to the steering wheel of his car, or post it on Facebook, making sure to tag him in the post.

♥ Write your husband a note, thanking him for something he did for you. It could be as simple as thanking him for working hard for your family, cutting the grass, or keeping up with your insurance.

♥ Put on a splash of body spray or his favorite perfume. Make sure he gets a good whiff of it before he leaves for work in the morning.

♥ Fill one helium balloon for each year you've been married. Attach a love note to the ribbon of each balloon. Place the balloons over your bed so when he comes into the room he sees the cloud of balloons with love notes hovering from the ceiling.

♥ Make him a little card the size of a credit card that says "Lifetime Member of the AAA Club of Marriage. I Admire, Adore, and Appreciate You." Slip it into his wallet.

♥ Make an intimate coupon booklet for your husband and put it in his underwear drawer. Get a simple small notepad, and tear off all but 26 sheets. Make the first sheet the cover sheet that says Coupon Booklet for My Man. On the next 25 sheets, write something you know he would love. You can repeat certain ideas you know he *really* loves. Ask him if he would like to redeem one of the coupons tonight.

Here's What the Guys Said

I appreciate getting compliments from people, but when Pam believes in me, I feel like I can conquer the world. Her words hold more weight and have more power to encourage because I value her so much. —Bill

The woman of my dreams is feminine and ladylike. She puts on makeup and is presentable when I get home, even if we don't have any place to go. My wife is really good at this. —Robert

The woman of my dreams is excited to see me every night when I come home from work. —Bob

My wife is always full of praise for me when I give her gifts or surprises. This makes me feel appreciated. —Dave

I've been shut up, shut down, shot down, ridiculed, disregarded, overlooked, overbooked, and overwhelmed…I know I was made for a reason. I know that, in God's eyes, I count. So, I simply want to find someone who believes in me. —Paul

DAY 4

Speaking Your Husband's Love Language

What says "love" to one person may not say "love" to another person. What says "romance" to one person may not say "romance" to another person. Dr. Gary Chapman, author of *The Five Love Languages*, suggests that we each have a certain "language" that speaks love.

1. Words of Affirmation: Compliments, words of encouragement, and requests rather than demands affirm the self-worth of your spouse. The man whose love language is words of affirmation feels loved by words that build him up.

2. Quality Time: Spending quality time together through sharing, listening, and participating in joint meaningful activities communicates that we truly care for and enjoy each other. The man whose love language is quality time feels loved when his wife wants to spend time with him.

3. Receiving Gifts: Gifts are tangible symbols of love, whether they are items you purchased or

made. Gifts demonstrate that you care, and they represent the value of the relationship. The man whose love language is receiving gifts feels loved when his wife gives him gifts both great and small.

4. Acts of Service: Cooking a meal, ironing a shirt, keeping the house clean, and paying the bills all speak volumes of love to the man whose love language is acts of service. If this is your man's love language, he will become frustrated when certain household duties go undone and will feel like a million bucks to sit down to his favorite meal. The man whose love language is acts of service will feel loved when his wife takes care of him and helps him with *his* to-do list.

5. Physical Touch: Physical touch is more than sexual. It is holding his hand, touching his shoulder, giving him a hug, patting his back, or snuggling next to him while watching TV. The man whose love language is physical touch feels loved when his wife is affectionate both privately and publicly.[1]

Go over the list with your husband and ask what says love to him. You may be surprised. You may think keeping the house clean or cooking yummy meals says love, when what he really wants is quality time or words of affirmation. If he can't tell you what his love language is, ask him what he longs for or wishes he had more of. You might be missing a simple small gesture that says "I love you" and wasting time on something that doesn't.

Here's another idea. Sit down with your husband and take the 5 Love Language profile quiz found at www.5lovelanguages .com/profile/couples. Print out a copy for him and a copy for you. After completing the quiz, ask your husband to guess your response to each question, and then you guess his response to each question.

> *What says "love" to one person may not say "love" to another person.*

Make it a point to really listen to what he has to say. *New York Times* bestselling author Stephen Covey noted, "Most people do not listen with the intent to understand; they listen with the intent to reply."[2] Don't worry about whether your husband is really getting what you're saying you need to feel loved. That would be nice, but remember, this is about understanding what you can do to make *him* feel loved. Hopefully he will learn something about his wife in the process, but keep your focus on listening to his heart and responding well.

Here's what Tiffany said about romancing her husband and focusing on his love language:

> My husband and I have been married almost 14 years and we have four children ranging from 6 to 12. His love language is encouragement and gifts,

mine is acts of service. I felt like a clean house and home-cooked meal made him feel loved, but I was wrong. I stink at thinking of ways to encourage and romance my husband. Actually, I thought I stunk at it until your challenge. I have realized that I just needed something to bring romance to the front of my mind first thing in the day, which made it easier to look for ways to make him feel special. He is a very happy camper and so am I!

And Debbie found that giving words of encouragement to her husband meant the world to him:

My husband was wowed by the 14-Day Romance Challenge! The first two days he asked me if it was the book I was reading that was making me extra loving (I got the Kindle version of *Becoming the Wife of His Dreams*. An awesome book—a must read). He wanted to send a special note of thanks to the author. The love note I wrote on his mirror is still there. He won't clean it off! His love language is words of affirmation and physical touch so he absolutely loved the emails and e-cards I sent. Thank you so much for the challenge.

Romance Challenge Ideas

♥ Ask your husband what makes him feel loved, and then add that to your priority list. Go over the five love languages with your husband and ask him what says love to him. (My husband wants me to stop what I'm doing when he gets home and give him a hug and a kiss. My tendency is to just keep working on what I'm doing. This one-minute reprieve from my busyness has blessed him.)

♥ String together an entire day of ways you can speak to him in his love language and get busy! See 10 Ways to Romance Your Husband According to His Love Language at the end of this book.

♥ Purchase several yummy scented candles for your bedroom and have them lit when he comes home from work or after dinner. Even if they are not lit, it will warm his heart to know you are thinking about him and planning ahead.

♥ Make him a coupon booklet with 100 coupons for 100 kisses. You can use a pack of sticky notes and write "coupon for a kiss" on each sheet of paper. Don't tear them apart; leave them intact.

♥ Sneak an article of sexy lingerie into his briefcase, in his work pants pocket, or on the seat of his car for a morning surprise. Don't be surprised if he comes home early!

Here's What the Guys Said

The biggest struggle in our marriage has been spiritual, emotional, and physical intimacy. She has a difficult time being vulnerable. —Richard

I wish my wife understood my inner life better: insecurity, embarrassment, shame, and hope. —Gene

I don't think there is anything my wife doesn't understand about me. We are able to openly talk about everything. —Nathan

DAY 5

Marveling at God's Divine Design

Have you ever stopped to think about the magnetism between a male and a female? Where did that come from? Why is it so strong? God put it there! Isn't He ingenious?

My paternal grandmother was a farm girl in the early 1900s. Much to her mortification, I asked her how she prevented having children without birth control. Her reply?

"I just didn't do the evil thing."

Oh my. "The evil thing," as Grandma Edwards called it, was created by God to be anything but evil. Sex was His idea! He took great care to make sexual relations between husband and wife pleasurable, desirable, and fulfilling. It is a sinful world that has taken God's holy design and perverted, exploited, and sullied it.

In Genesis 2 we read, "The LORD God formed a man from the dust of the ground and breathed into his nostrils the breath of life, and the man became a living being" (v. 7). "The LORD God said, 'It is not good for the man to be alone. I will make a helper suitable for him…So the LORD God caused the man to fall into a deep sleep; and while he was sleeping, he took one of the man's ribs and then closed up the place with flesh. Then the LORD God made a woman from the rib he had taken out of the man" (vv. 21-22).

Now, stop the cameras on this scene and let's use our imaginations for a moment. When we think of creation, we tend to think of the big picture: land and sea, sun and moon, creeping animals and swarming seas. But I want us to turn our attention to the intricacies of the human body, features that were made not by the hand of God, but by the fingertips of God. The eyes, hair follicles, sweat glands, salivary glands, capillaries, eyebrows, cilia lining the nose, staple bone in the inner ear, wrinkles of skin on the knuckles, toenails, and bumps on the tongue. Now, think of all God fashioned for the sexual union of man and woman. Girlfriend, God created a lot simply for pleasure. Wow! What a thought.

Let's envision God having a show-and-tell for the angels just before He woke Adam and Eve from their deep sleep. As the angels circled around the sleeping pair, God stood over His works of art to point out some of their unique features.

"Each aspect of these creations has a unique function crafted for a specific purpose," God explained. "Let's start at the top and work our way down."

God then explained how the hard skull served to encase the much softer brain just below the surface and pointed out the specific function of each of the 206 bones of the body. He showed the angels how fingerlike nerve endings sent signals to the brain, how the heart pumped blood through veins, arteries, and capillaries like an ocean feeding rivers, streams, and tributaries, and how food would be taken into the mouth, flow down the esophagus to the stomach and then filter through the small and large intestines. For hours God excitedly pointed out one intriguing, intricate detail after another. Finally, God reached just below the male and female waists where the organs for sexual reproduction are housed. "You'll find this very interesting," He said with great enthusiasm.

He first turned their attention to the male and showed the angels the tiny tubes where life-giving semen is created, stored, and released. "Every 48 hours or so, semen will build up and scream to be released. When properly stimulated by the woman, blood will fill the man's penis. When the stimulation is conduced, the semen, filled with microscopic sperm, will shoot forth with the force of a geyser and enter the woman. If one sperm reaches an egg and breaks through the protective covering, they will be joined just as the man and woman are joined, and new life will begin."

"How does the stimulation occur?" asked an angel.

"This fleshy tissue you see lying here just between the man's legs is extremely sensitive to the touch. I have concentrated 17 sexual glands in this one area. The most sensitive part is the underside of the shaft and the head. The ridge on the bottom of the head and the indentation you see here on that ridge is hypersensitive."

"But God," the angels said, "it is so flexible. How will it ever have the strength to enter into the female?"

"The penis may not look like much to you right now, but when the man's wife touches him, it will be quite a different story."

"Amazing," they all agreed.

"But what about the woman?" one of the angels inquired. "She is very different."

"Yes," the Lord said. "She is created as the receptor for the man."

Then God explained how He worked with His fingertips to create the glove type opening for the man's penis. He demonstrated how He scooped out an area that would receive the man and then went about meticulously creating other fascinating features.

God pointed out the ovaries where the eggs are created and the fallopian tubes where the eggs travel down to the uterus. He showed them the vagina and its placement just behind the urethra.

"You'll notice this fleshy knob of tissue just above the opening of the vagina. There are actually two sets, an outer and an inner set of fleshy lips. These are called labia. The outer labia are covered with hair, but the inner labia are not. Then right here is an extra sensitive area called the clitoris. It's hard to see, but it's at the hood of the inner labia. When the man stimulates this area, she will feel intense pleasure."

"It's so small," an angel mused. "How will the husband ever find it?"

"It may take some practice. But if he's smart, he'll search until he does. It's kind of like a treasure hunt! Just like the penis, when the clitoris is stimulated, it becomes larger and easier to find. It will actually protrude just a bit from hiding in the folds of the labia. What you see here is only the tip of the iceberg. The clitoris is about nine inches long and is nestled inside the woman's body, making the entire area sensitive to touch. However, when her husband touches her in the hypersensitive area, that iceberg will begin to melt and she will experience waves of ecstasy that will run through her entire body. The clitoris, like the penis, is very sensitive to touch and is the center of exquisite pleasure when handled properly or intense pain when handled improperly.

"Also, there's another secret spot just inside the woman's vagina opening on the front wall. When that is stimulated by the man, she will experience extreme arousal and eventual waves of ecstasy."

"But God, it seems You have put a lot of detail and attention into the sensory component of the reproduction process for humans. I don't recall that for the other animals You have created," one of the angels noted.

"You are quite right," God responded. "I have gone to great lengths to create the intricate parts of both male and female reproductive organs. The sexual act for a husband and wife is not simply for reproduction. I have fashioned many sensitive areas for one purpose only—pleasure. This is My gift to them. Pleasure is not necessary for reproduction. I created them this way because I love them."

The human anatomy designed for sexual pleasure was created by a loving God.

After God finished pointing out the other incredible intricacies of both the man and the woman, He breathed a strong wind over their bodies and stirred them awake.

Up to this point, we have no recorded words from the man Adam, but after he laid eyes on the fair Eve, he said, "Whoa. Now, this is good!" That's not exactly what he said, but that's what he meant. He said, "This is now bone of my bones and flesh of my flesh; she shall be called 'woman,' for she was taken out of man" (Genesis 2:23).

Are you blushing? I think it may be worth it. What I want you to realize is that the human anatomy designed for sexual pleasure was created by a loving God. He formed you and your husband to give pleasure to and receive pleasure from one another. Many facets of the human body serve no other purpose. Science has shown us that all you need to make a baby is joining an egg with one tiny, determined sperm. You can do that in a petri dish in a laboratory. However, to make love, you need a lot more.

According to Linda Dillow and Lorraine Pintus, authors of *Intimate Issues*, "The Hebrew word for 'sexual intercourse' is the word 'to know.' Through God's gift of sex, a husband and wife receive an intimate knowing of one another that they have with no one else."[1] Ingenious!

God created sex. Doesn't that tell you a lot about who He really is? Among other things, it tells you He is a creative marvel with infinite artistic flair.

Are you having fun? Is your husband starting to wonder what's up? Here's what a couple of your sisters had to say about what the challenge did for their marriage:

On the fourth day my husband said, "You have been awfully nice to me lately." I just chuckled and said, "It's about time, huh?" It has been a great 14 days. He called me by a "pet" name, which doesn't typically happen, and was even more compassionate and understanding than usual. In the hustle of raising two teens and busily keeping up with their lives, I had forgotten to treasure the one who gave me those two and whom I will have even when they leave the house. Thanks for the challenge!

I'm so close to tears as I write this comment. My husband just sent me the sweetest email thanking me for surprising him with a sweet, creative evening. I must admit our romance department was suffering, but this challenge woke me up. And finally this morning I saw a glint in my husband's eyes. Our love has been renewed, and it's really been overwhelming. He is a good man and deserves the best of me, and that's what I'll give him all the days of my life.

Romance Challenge Ideas

♥ Warm up your husband's socks in the dryer and have them waiting for him when he gets out of the shower with a note that says, "You warm my heart."

♥ Warm up a blanket in the dryer and go out to watch the sunrise together.

♥ Hire someone to do his least favorite household chore for one week. For example, hire someone to mow the lawn, rake the leaves, or shovel snow off the sidewalk.

♥ Make a list of a few of your husband's body parts and tell him what you love about each one. Use your fingers and hands to point them out.

♥ Give your husband a full body massage with oils or lotion and tell him what you like about each part. Save the best for last and let him know you love how that part works.

Here's What the Guys Said

I wish my wife would initiate sexual intimacy more often. I've read the books where I should start the whole day to get her thinking about it and looking forward to it, but it sure would be nice if she was the one who initiated it. —Brent

What is one thing I wish my wife understood better about me and what I long for? The need for her to be more sexual. I wish she'd be more creative and enthusiastic about it. I wish sex would be more fun and more of a priority in our marriage. —Rod

The woman of my dreams would want sex as much as I do. I don't think women really have a concept of how "wired" for sex men are. It can't make sense to them—not exactly sure why myself. It seems petty, but it's real. Also, the woman of my dreams would be confident in who she is, love the Lord deeply, and challenge me. —Aaron

Making Marriage a Priority

A best practice is to maintain cars by getting them serviced every 5000 miles or according to the manufacturer's recommendations, but some people just drive them until they fall apart. A best practice is to have teeth cleaned and examined every six to twelve months, but some people ignore them until they fall out. And a best practice is to make marriage a priority and take steps to keep it strong, but some take it for granted or neglect it until it fizzles out. The fact that you are holding this book in your hand lets me know you are not that person.

We all can get so busy just taking care of the daily routine that we let sexual intimacy get pushed down the priority list. Cliff and Joyce Penner interviewed several thousand people before writing their book *The Gift of Sex*. They discovered that 75 percent said lack of time was the greatest frustration in their sex life.[1] So here's the deal: we need to make time.

If necessary, put lovemaking on your calendar. I imagine you have hair appointments, doctor appointments, and children's activities on the calendar, so why not include your number one priority—your marriage and your man. I know we would like to think intimacy is always a spontaneous, passionate, raucous tryst. After all, isn't that what we see on television and the silver screen? But that's not real life. Most days are just daily, and we have to plan ahead…sometimes.

If putting lovemaking on the schedule seems unromantic to you, consider these positive aspects of scheduled intimacy:

Scheduled Intimacy Eliminates the Possibility of Rejection.

In most marriages one partner has a higher sex drive than the other. For the spouse with the higher desire, the fear of rejection can be highly detrimental to self-image, self-esteem, and overall unity in the marriage.

Did you know most men find initiating sex one of the riskiest ventures they ever make? Each time a man initiates sex, he knows he is risking rejection. When he is rejected often enough, he internalizes his hurt and disappointment and often becomes angry. This can lead to several reactions—none of them good. He may give up, be tempted to look elsewhere, or seek female affirmation outside his own home. Having a scheduled day for intimacy eliminates "the ask," which takes the stress of asking out of the equation.

> *When it comes to sex, women are like Crock-Pots and men are like microwaves.*

Scheduled Intimacy Increases Desire and Anticipation.

The largest sex organ in the human body is the brain.

Anticipating intimacy at the end of a certain day gets the mind in gear and jump-starts the process. If one spouse has a lower sex drive than the other, a reminder on the calendar might be just the ticket to prepare the mind and body. I've often heard that when it comes to sex, women are like Crock-Pots and men are like microwaves. So if you are the Crock-Pot, make sure to plug it in and let the romantic juices simmer throughout the day.

Scheduled Intimacy Ensures That Too Much Time Doesn't Pass.

No matter what is going on in your life, don't allow too much time pass between times of sexual intimacy. The longer the period between coming together, the more difficult it is to even begin. I read a lot of studies, and most agree that having sex at least once a week is a good rule of thumb to maintain a healthy marriage.[2][3] If you write it on your calendar, you will make sure other activates are not crowding out time for sexual intimacy.

Having lovemaking on your calendar isn't for everyone. I dare say it's not necessary for most. But if you find too much time is passing between times of sexual intimacy or your husband is frustrated because you are too tired more often than not, it is something to consider.

That doesn't mean you can't have sex on nonscheduled days, but it might serve as a reminder that a certain number of days have passed. The longer you wait, the more difficult it is to get mentally, emotionally, and physically prepared. You might think that is the other way around, but it's not. Couples who have sex regularly are happier and more connected.

In the book of Proverbs, King Solomon tells his son the joys of having sexual relations with the same woman for his entire life. "Drink water from your own cistern, and running water from your own well. Should your fountains be dispersed abroad, streams of water in the streets? Let them be only your own, and not for strangers with you. Let your fountain be blessed, and rejoice with the wife of our youth. As a loving deer and a graceful doe, let her breasts satisfy you at all times; and always be enraptured with her love" (Proverbs 5:15-19 NKJV). That's great advice, but if the man goes to the well and the well is dry, he might be tempted to dip his cup elsewhere to quench his thirst.

In his book *Sheet Music*, Dr. Kevin Leman notes, "Instead of resenting requests to stop by the store or take a look at a leaky faucet, a sexually fulfilled man will jump with eagerness. Instead of being cold and distant when you talk to him, he's going to want to hear what you have to say."[4]

Dr. Leman also notes the following:

> Some wives reading this may be thinking, I tried that, and it didn't work. Such a response shows me that you're misunderstanding me entirely. You can't just "try" this; it has to become a way of life. One good time of sex will make a man thankful— for a while. But if he's turned down the next five times he approaches you, he'll think about the five rejections, not that one special night.
>
> Because of a man's chemical makeup, sex feels like

a need to most of us, and when a woman graciously and eagerly meets that need, we become very thankful. When a woman uses a man's need to manipulate him, a man becomes resentful. When a woman uses a man's need to punish him, he often becomes bitter.[5]

> *When a wife withholds sex as a weapon for manipulation, it will boomerang and come right back to her—aimed directly at the heart.*

It all goes back to the reasons why we want to romance our husbands in the first place. Is it to give or to get? Oh, believe me, when you give in this area of his life, you will indeed reap many wonderful benefits. However, if you are giving in this area only to get, he will be able to tell—and so will God. Remember, the Bible warns us that wrong motives will leave us empty (James 4:6).

When a wife refuses her husband sexually, she shouldn't be surprised when he refuses her practically (like fixing that leaky faucet or running to the store). When she withholds sex as a weapon for manipulation, it will boomerang and come right back to her—aimed directly at the heart.

Proverbs 13:12 tells us that "hope deferred makes the heart sick." We've all seen it. Your husband comes slinking into the bathroom as you're washing your face getting ready for bed.

He has that sheepish grin you know so well, slides his hand around your waist, and says, "You tired?"

"Yep, sure am," you quickly reply.

The next look you see in the mirror from that man standing behind you? That is hope deferred personified. Now, if his advances are dashed enough times, hope deferred becomes hope destroyed.

> *Marriage is a decision to serve*
> *the other, whether in bed or out.*

Let's look at what the Bible has to say about our right of refusal, for the husband and the wife.

> The husband should fulfill his marital duty to his wife, and likewise the wife to her husband. The wife does not have authority over her own body but yields it to her husband. In the same way, the husband does not have authority over his own body but yields it to his wife. Do not deprive each other except perhaps by mutual consent and for a time, so that you may devote yourselves to prayer. Then come together again so that Satan will not tempt you because of your lack of self control (1 Corinthians 7:3-5).

Now take a look at this same passage in Eugene Peterson's paraphrase in The Message:

It's good for a man to have a wife, and for a woman to have a husband. Sexual drives are strong, but marriage is strong enough to contain them and provide for a balanced and fulfilling sexual life in a world of sexual disorder. The marriage bed must be a place of mutuality—the husband seeking to satisfy his wife, the wife seeking to satisfy her husband. Marriage is not a place to "stand up for your rights." Marriage is a decision to serve the other, whether in bed or out. Abstaining from sex is permissible for a period of time if you both agree to it, and if it's for the purposes of prayer and fasting—but only for such times. Then come back together again. Satan has an ingenious way of tempting us when we least expect it. I'm not, understand, commanding these periods of abstinence—only providing my best counsel if you should choose them.

> *Saying "I do" at the altar means we're committing to say "I will" in the bedroom.*

If ever there was a politically incorrect statement, this is one of them: "The wife does not have authority over her own body." But Paul is saying our bodies are not to do with as we please. Saying "I do" at the altar means we're committing to say "I will" in the bedroom. And the same goes for the husband.

Proverbs 31:12 tells us that the wife of noble character does her husband "good, not harm" all the days of her life. When we deny our husbands sexually, we are, in a sense, leading them into temptation. Paul tells us right there in 1 Corinthians that when we deny our man, we are tempting him to look elsewhere. We are opening the door to Satan, and he is all too ready to pounce right in and devour.

I don't know about you, but that thought brings terror to my heart. That is the fright of refusal. Could I actually be tempting my husband to sin by denying him sexually? Yes. If we are not fulfilling our husbands sexually, we are asking for trouble. This type of action or I should say, lack of action, on our part will cloud his thinking, discourage his manhood, and encourage him to look elsewhere.

By our willingness to fulfill our husband sexually, we can make him feel like the luckiest man on earth. On the other hand, by our constant rejection of his advances, we can make him feel defeated and deflated. We have a choice as to how we will make him feel: elated or emasculated, blessed or cursed, top dog or underdog. God has given us wives a lot of power! He must have thought we could handle it. How are you doing in this area?

Let's get down to the business of making our marriage and our man a top priority.

Romance Challenge Ideas

♥ Put a note that says, "I love you" in his coffee cup the night before and place it by the coffeemaker.

If he's not a coffee drinker, put the note in a cereal bowl or juice glass.

♥ Write him a love letter. If you'd like a little help crafting it, see "10 Easy Steps to Writing a Love Letter" at the end of this book.

♥ Surprise him with a date night. Make all the arrangements, including dinner reservations, a fun activity (such as a movie or dancing), and a dessert that only you can provide. Make sure to not talk about problems or the children.

♥ Go by his workplace and slip a "ticket" under his windshield wiper. Write the following: "You have been cited for being the sexiest man in the world. There is no fine, because you are so fine." Sign it "Officer (your first name)."

♥ Okay, let's spice that last idea up a little. Go by his workplace and slip a note under his windshield wiper. Write the following: "Would the owner of this car please report to (your address) to meet your lover for a romantic rendezvous?" Make sure the kids are at a friend's house for a couple of hours or for the night. Perhaps switch off with a friend and then keep her kids while she puts a similar note on her husband's windshield.

Here's What the Guys Said

I wish my wife understood my need and desire for her companionship in activities I enjoy. —Terry

My wife is really good at taking interest in what interests me—like sports. —Carter

One thing I wish my wife understood is that I feel her relationship with God is the most important thing. Also, it is a lot easier to go the extra mile for what is most important to her when our sexual relationship is healthy. —Ben

DAY 7

Keeping Hubby First

The woman of your man's dreams makes him number one above every other human relationship—above her parents, above the children, and above all others. She safeguards her marriage against the inevitable forces that threaten to wedge their way between her and her husband and stands as a sentry to protect them against anything that would pry them apart.

One of the men who completed my survey said, "The wife of my dreams lets me know, in a way I understand, that next to God, I'm the most important person in her life."

Among the most common problems in marriages today are issues related to sex, money, and in-laws. Mother-in-law jokes are plentiful, but in-law problems are no laughing matter. While there is no ample supply of verses in the Bible concerning extended family, there is one primary directive: "A man shall leave his father and his mother, and shall cleave to his wife: and they shall be one flesh" (Genesis 2:24 NKJV). I find it interesting that God gave this instruction before there was even a mother and father to leave. God sees past, present, and future all at once, and He knew the problems that could arise from the refusal of men and women to leave their parents and cleave to their marriage partners.

A wise wife safeguards her marriage against the inevitable forces that threaten to wedge their way between her and her husband and stands as a sentry to protect them against anything that would pry them apart.

When Steve and I had been married for about five years, we sat down and made some ground rules on how to deal with extended family. And while those boundaries upset in-laws on both sides, they served us well in keeping our marriage a priority. I only wish it hadn't taken five years for us to figure out that we needed to set those boundaries. We could have avoided a lot of heartache.

When it comes to extended family, several questions need to be addressed. How often do we visit? How long do we stay? How long do the in-laws stay when they come to visit? Where do we spend Christmas or Thanksgiving? Do we spend vacation time with extended family? How much do we tell extended family about our finances? Our marital struggles? Our parenting decisions?

Questions such as these can be difficult to agree upon, but it's important to reach an agreement before the problem is staring you in the face (or knocking on the door). It might be a difficult discussion, but it's a way to let your husband know he's the most important person on earth to you, and second only to God.

The key is to reach an agreement you are both comfortable with and that will honor your spouse. Remember, the most important family unit God has ordained in your life is you and your husband.

God does call us to honor our fathers and mothers. Moses wrote, "Honor your father and mother. Then you will live a long, full life in the land the Lord your God is giving you" (Exodus 20:12 NLT). This is the only commandment with a promise of future blessing.

Author Sandra Aldrich wrote, "Honoring does not mean letting them order you around, pry into your personal finances, tell your kids to get haircuts, or rearrange your cabinets each time they visit. It means honoring their position. Once the child becomes an adult, it's important that a new relationship be built—more 'friend to friend' than 'parent to child.'"[1]

But what about when the kids start coming? What then?

Do you remember that old childhood chant, "First comes love, then comes marriage, then comes Susie with the baby carriage"? Did you ever wonder why there wasn't a second verse? I've watched what happens to couples after the babies start to come. Too many times a husband gets pushed out of his first-place position and has to resign himself to playing second fiddle. Obviously, a child requires more time and energy than a grown man, but a skillful wife assures her guy he is still number one in her heart.

Rob Parsons, author of *The Sixty Minute Marriage Builder*, wrote about the adjustment his marriage went through after the birth of their first child.

I have sympathy for the person who said, "Insanity

is hereditary—you get it from your kids!" I don't think I could love my children more, but why didn't anybody warn my wife and me of the changes they were going to cause in our relationship? One minute Diane and I were spending our evenings taking walks together, visiting friends, and reading in front of the fire. The next we were walking the halls at midnight singing nursery rhymes and dealing with postpartum depression—in me![2]

A mother should never feel guilty for putting her husband before her children. Growing up in a difficult home, where my parents vacillated between heated arguments and passive-aggressive silence, I would have given anything to know they loved each other—that my daddy was Mom's priority. Giving your children the security of knowing their parents love each other is one of the best gifts you can give them.

Most likely your man is not going to express his disappointment about playing second fiddle to the children. But, friend, he told me. Maybe not your husband, but hundreds just like him.

I wish my wife and I spent more time together without the kids. —Randy

What is one thing my wife does well? She cares for the children (sometimes too much). —Matt

I wish my wife understood my need to be her first

> *priority, after Jesus and BEFORE the kids or other*
> *outside interests.* —Craig

And then there's the comment from this man about how his wife went the extra mile to make sure he knew he was number one.

> *My wife and I have been married for more than 12*
> *years. During this time we've had three children and*
> *have gone through periods where she worked outside*
> *the home or stayed with the children. For the entire*
> *period, she has not failed to wake up early in the*
> *morning to spend time with me and fix me break-*
> *fast before I go to work. This has meant a lot to me.*
> —Travis

Dr. John Roseman noted, "Today's typical wife, as soon as she becomes a parent, begins to act as if she took a marriage vow that read, 'I take you to be my husband, until children do us part.'"[3]

I can remember a time, and not too long ago, when a wife who became a mother remained first and foremost a wife. A woman who worked outside the home was referred to as a "working wife" and a woman who worked in the home was referred to as a "housewife."

But a paradigm shift has occurred in our way of thinking, which is reflected in the terms we use to describe a woman's employment status. Today's woman in the same circumstances is referred to as a "working mom" or a "stay-at-home mom."

Now, some might think that is an improvement. After all, who wants to be married to their house? But I think the change is more a reflection of a cultural shift of importance from being a wife to that of being a mother. Our focus has shifted from a home centered on the marriage unit to one centered on the children. That concerns me.

It has been said that sex makes little kids, and kids make little sex. One way or another, having children will affect your marriage. Don't let that new little man in your life dethrone the ruling king. And make sure that little princess who stole your husband's heart knows you are still the queen.

Here's what three women said happened in their homes when they decided to put Daddy first.

> It has been wonderful and a great reminder that it doesn't take that much time out of the day to place my husband back into priority number one. With having three kids five and under, it is easy for my husband to be pushed aside. Also as a mother, I feel like I have put a "lid" on the sexy side of me. This helped to rekindle that confidence and not be afraid to show my husband that the woman he married six-and-a-half years and three kids later still lives inside me.

> I thought putting my kids first and taking care of everything at home such as the cooking and the cleaning was good enough, but I found out I was wrong. In the challenge I was forced to put my

husband before the kids. My husband was really surprised at the notes left for him. On the morning I heated up his towel, he thought I was playing a joke, and it made me think about the ways I was failing him. I shocked him when I rented a hotel and had candles, chocolate dipped strawberries, and a sexy outfit. I blindfolded him, and he was totally shocked and surprised. He loved the time away from the kids and so did I!

I had the husband-child order all wrong. I thought kids came first. Since taking the challenge, which at first felt weird, it made me see my husband in a new light. I forgot the man I fell in love with and was just seeing another man to take care of along with the boys. I feel better for knowing that my husband is satisfied and that it's okay to initiate sex and have fun with it—things we as parents had forgotten how to do.

So get busy and make sure your husband knows he is number one in your heart.

Romance Challenge Ideas

♥ Text your husband a love note with a hashtag such as #crazyaboutmyman, #crazyinlove, #hunkyhusband, or #happywife.

♥ Sneak his car to the car wash. Then leave a note on the steering wheel that says, "I love you. Enjoy your clean car today!"

♥ Purchase a bottle of the cologne he wore when you were dating and give it to him as a surprise. Just the idea that you remembered it will stir his heart. He'll feel like Romeo just putting it on.

♥ Spray your sheets and pillows with a soft, yummy fragrance. Turn down the sheets and sprinkle a few flower petals.

♥ Make reservations at a hotel for just the two of you. Give your husband a note that says, "I want you all to myself." Don't talk about the kids for at least 24 hours.

Here's What the Guys Said

The greatest struggle in our marriage has been arguments about the children. —Russ

What is one thing my wife does well? She is a great mom. —Joe

I wish my wife would give me the same amount of quality time and attention she gives everybody else. —Dave

My wife shows great respect by not taking any disagreements we have beyond us. She doesn't bring her mom or friends in on it. She protects our marriage in this way. —Justin

DAY 8

Applying the Superglue of Marriage

When I interviewed and surveyed men for *Becoming the Woman of His Dreams*, you can believe sexual fulfillment was at the top of their list. No surprise there. As a matter-of-fact, it was first and foremost, running neck and neck with respect.

> *Sexual fulfillment is not just the glue of marriage. It's the superglue.*

Sexual fulfillment is climactic in a man's life—pun intended. If you excel in praying for him, respecting him, adoring him, initiating intimate friendship, safeguarding your marriage, and encouraging him, but neglect sexually fulfilling him, all your efforts will be for naught. Sexual fulfillment is the glue that holds all the other elements together.

It's not just the glue of marriage. It's the superglue.

Dr. Kevin Leman has counseled thousands of couples and

has determined that a couple's sex life is a microcosm of the marriage. If the sex life is good, then the marriage is good. Very rarely does he see a bad marriage with a good sex life.[1]

If your husband is sexually fulfilled, he will race a train, take a bullet, and climb the highest mountain to make sure you are okay. He will be a better father, better provider, better employee, and even a better sportsman. That's right—sportsman. *Sports Illustrated* reported that behind every MVP is a good woman—and just one. Happily married men make better baseball players![2] (By the way, how did I know this? I entered into my husband's world and read an article in his magazine.)

This is what Dr. Leman has to say about the sexually fulfilled husband.

> A sexually fulfilled husband will do anything for you. Sex is such a basic need for men that when this area of their life is well taken care of, they feel immense appreciation and act accordingly. A sexually fulfilled man is the kind who drives to work thinking, *I'm so glad I married that woman. I must be the happiest man alive!* And who then drives home thinking, *What special thing can I do for my wife this evening?* If you want this kind of loyalty and appreciation, meet your husband's sexual needs; no other need generates such deep thankfulness.[3]

Bill Farrel, who authored the book *Red-Hot Monogamy*

with his wife, Pam, said this about how romance and sexual intimacy affected other areas of his life:

> It amazes me that, after 25 years of being together, sex still has such an effect on Pam and me. When we are in sync with each other and enjoying each other often, life is good. The sky is bluer, the sun is brighter, and all tasks seem easier. I know I am easily distracted by Pam when we are in tune with each other, but I accomplish more in the other areas of my life. I think more clearly and have more emotional energy to invest in my goals... I freeze in my tracks when she winks at me and gives me that "Do you wanna?" look. It takes time out of my schedule, but I still get more done. I will never understand that.
>
> It also amazes me to know how ridiculous I can be when we are not as sexually active as I would like. I become sad, frustrated, and even angry. I snap at dumb things in life and become unproductive. Everything seems harder and less interesting. I find myself thinking weird thoughts, such as: *I thought she cared about me. She used to think I was attractive. Why is everything else in life more important than me?* To be sure, these are overreactions, but I don't seem to have any defenses against thinking this way, except of course, reengaging sexually with Pam.[4]

> *Sexual intimacy soothes his accumulated soul aches from the day and gives your husband the strength and well-being necessary to face the world with confidence.*

In his book *Love and Respect,* Dr. Emerson Eggerichs wrote,

> [Your husband] needs sexual release as you need emotional release. This is why he loves the act of sex in and of itself…As a woman, you may feel that the two of you have to feel and be close in order to share sexually. For him, however, it is the reverse; the sexual act is what brings the two of you close![5]

Making love with your husband assures him that you find him desirable and that he's still "got what it takes." Sexual intimacy soothes his accumulated soul aches from the day and gives him the strength and well-being necessary to face the world with confidence. And, of course, sex also makes him feel loved—in fact, he can't feel completely loved without it.

Here's what a few of the women had to say about what happened when they spiced up their sex life:

> When I met my husband with a hot towel and cocoa he said, "Can I marry you?" When I wrote on the bathroom mirror he smiled all day! But when I made him a coupon booklet… Let's just say it was his FAVORITE! In fact he liked it so much I'm going to make him one every Valentine's Day, on our anniversary, and on his birthday!

God has used this 14-Day Challenge to save my marriage and add 50 more years to our romance. My husband is so grateful for me, and I'm grateful for the challenge. It was the most rewarding challenge I have ever done. My friends were so amazed at the ideas, they started to do them too. My husband went to bed every night with a smile and woke up with a smile. I'm even blushing.

One day I stole all my husband's underwear and left his tuxedo underwear (from our honeymoon) and a bow tie in his drawer. He went off to work with a smile and an old pair of undies but he knew what was waiting for him when he got home!

Romance Challenge Ideas

♥ Send your husband a love note to his work email.

♥ Have his favorite music playing when he comes home from work. If he gets home before you do, put a CD in the CD player and put a note on the door that says, "Press 'Play' on the CD player and enjoy."

♥ Serve your husband breakfast in bed.

♥ Buy him some sexy underwear.

♥ Ask your husband the following questions:

- What part of your body do you enjoy me touching the most?
- What scent puts you in the mood?
- What sort of lighting do you enjoy during times of intimacy?
- In what sort of packaging would you like for me to present myself?
- What do you like for me to wear?

♥ Take notes. Then put meeting his desires into practice.

Here's What the Guys Said

Women often trivialize men's sexual needs. I know too many men in dangerous situations because of this. —Steven

I wish my wife understood my desire is to make sex last longer with more foreplay. Our greatest struggle has been the quality of our sex life. —Will

On a scale of 1 to 10, sexual fulfillment for me rates at 11. —Chris

DAY 9

Recharging His Battery

I work hard all day," Jim explains. "When I come home, my greatest desire is to be recharged so I can go back out and do it all again the next day. What I wish my wife understood is that sex recharges me. She acts like it is a drain, but I wish she understood that when I'm left unfulfilled, it's like going to work with an empty tank."

What recharges your battery? Shopping? Coffee with friends? Rest? Time alone? A pedicure? A spiritual retreat?

Guess what recharges your husband's battery? You guessed it. Sex. If your husband is under stress because a project is due next week, one of the best gifts you can give him is to recharge his battery by making love and giving him the confidence he needs. Did his boss chew him out today? Did he lose that big order? Did he miss a deadline? Did he have to confront a coworker? Many events in a man's day can drain his emotional battery. Sex with the wife of his dreams is God's unique physical and mental therapy prescription.

A man who is sexually fulfilled by the wife of his dreams
will feel great about himself. He may not be king of the hill
at the office, but if he knows he is the king of the hill in the
bedroom, he'll keep a smile on his face and a skip in his step.

Dr. John Gray explained it this way:

> Many times after having great sex with my wife, I
> realize that I had forgotten how beautiful the trees
> are in our neighborhood. I go outside and breathe
> in the fresh air and feel alive again. It is not that
> I didn't feel alive in my work, but by connecting
> with my wife through great sex, I can reawaken
> and bring my more sensual feelings that are easily
> forgotten in the focused pursuit of achieving my
> goals at work. In a sense, great sex helps me stop
> and smell the flowers.[1]

Sex is one of the most effective ways you can encourage
and minister to your husband. Physical intimacy with the wife
of his dreams assures him that he is still desirable and very
much a man.

A man who is sexually fulfilled by the wife of his dreams
will feel great about himself. He may not be king of the hill at
the office, but if he knows he is the king of the hill in the bedroom, he'll keep a smile on his face and a skip in his step.

Not only does making love with you recharge your husband's battery, but it is just plain good for his health! And the

more energy you put into romancing him, the more you will be fulfilled yourself. Putting a love note on the rearview mirror of his car makes you feel good. As you read the comments of women who have already taken the challenge, you will notice many mentioned the change they saw in their own hearts.

> *Romancing your husband is not only good for your marriage; it's great for both your and your husband's overall health and well-being.*

Here's a little physiology lesson. In a 2006 study, Jorge Moll and colleagues at the National Institutes of Health found that when people give to charities, it activates regions of the brain associated with pleasure, social connection, and trust, creating a "warm glow" effect. Scientists also believe altruistic behavior releases endorphins in the brain, producing the positive feeling known as the "helper's high."[2]

Romancing your husband affects the same areas of your brain that creates those endorphins to give you that "helper's high." Isn't it interesting that when God created woman, He said, "I will make a helper suitable for him" (Genesis 2:18)? As you give yourself to your husband, you can have that same "helper's high." And a bonus is that romancing him gives his endorphins a super lift.

Another study showed the following:

> Giving has also been linked to the release of oxytocin, a hormone (also released during sex and

breast feeding) that induces feelings of warmth, euphoria, and connection to others. In laboratory studies, Paul Zak, the director of the Center for Neuroeconomic Studies at Claremont Graduate University, has found that a dose of oxytocin will cause people to give more generously and to feel more empathy towards others, with "symptoms" lasting up to two hours. And those people on an "oxytocin high" can potentially jumpstart a "virtuous circle," where one person's generous behavior triggers another's.[3]

I really like the idea of a virtuous cycle of giving!

Another study showed that flirting releases endorphins.[4] So when you romance your husband by doing something as small as leaving a love note on his windshield, or writing "I love you" on his bathroom mirror, it makes *you* feel good! It releases endorphins—the feel good biochemical that affects your mood and creates a vibe of happiness and well-being. Bottom line, romancing your husband is not only good for your marriage; it's great for both your and your husband's overall health and well-being.

In their book *Intended for Pleasure*, Ed and Gaye Wheat write, "Today therapists and researchers are discovering that genuine sexual intimacy has a remarkable power to heal, renew, refresh, restore, and sustain the marriage relationship."[5]

It recharges your husband's battery…and it recharges yours.

Here's what two participants in the 14-Day Challenge noticed:

> My husband and I have been married for 12 years.
> It has been a good marriage, but somewhere along
> the way I stopped making romance a top priority.
> The 14-Day Romance Challenge sparked my cre-
> ativity and desire to romance my husband as I first
> did in the early years of our marriage. After focus-
> ing on my husband for 14 days in a row, he said
> he feels empowered, adored, and valued. It is an
> answer to my prayers for him and myself...that
> God would show me how to love and pursue my
> husband as He pursues us. Thank you for spark-
> ing a fire and glory to God for fanning the flames!

> During the first few days, I realized I hadn't been
> putting enough focus on my husband. By focus-
> ing on him, I actually began to have those sweet,
> wonderful affectionate feelings that I hadn't felt
> for a long time while raising kids, doing house-
> work, volunteering at church, and going to work.
> We have a great marriage, but this seemed to put
> back a lot of the sweetness and attention that had
> faded. I did a "You are wonderful because..." card
> for the 14 days and he loved finding them. He
> always had a huge grin on his face after he read
> them. My husband is very happy, especially after
> "fulfilling his needs" twice in one day! I didn't

expect it, but he has been so attentive to me the past two weeks. We are like honeymooners again.

So let's recharge that battery and get the positive energy flowing.

Romance Challenge Ideas

♥ Ask your husband how you can pray for him today. That will let him know you love and care for him.

♥ Buy him a pack of batteries. Take them out of the package and tie cute bows around them. Attach a note that says, "You recharge my battery."

♥ Purchase a key at a hardware store. Look for one in a great color, such as red or blue. Loop a ribbon, piece of twine, or small rope through it and attach a note that reads, "You hold the key to my heart."

♥ Put a pack of Red Hots candy on his car seat with a note that says, "Saw these at the store today and thought of you!"

♥ Put a note on your bed like the ones restaurants put on a reserved table that says "RESERVED." When he asks what it's for, tell him you've made a reservation for a special rendezvous at _____. You fill in the time.

Here's What the Guys Said

*A man dreams of being needed and wanted by a wife.
There are times when I know my wife looks up to me,
respects me, and honors me. That is when I love her
the most, and when I feel the best about myself as well.
When I feel strong, I am strong. More than any other
person in the world, she holds the key to my confidence.*
—Al

*What is the one thing I wish the woman of my dreams
understood about me? Sex.* —Gene

*Our greatest struggle has been physical intimacy. I believe
that we need to work together, perhaps even through
counseling, to move forward together on this.* —Andy

Letting Him Know
You Want Him!

You're on Day 10! Congratulations! I'm so excited for you!

Now, let's chat a little bit about a woman's "wifely duty," as I've heard it referred to more times than I can count.

A woman who fulfills her "wifely duty" out of obligation does not produce a sexually fulfilled husband. Nope, not at all. If you are having sex because you feel like you *have to* rather than making love because you *want to*, your husband can tell. Think of it this way. How would you feel if your husband came home from work on your anniversary, handed you a dozen roses, and said, "I didn't really want to get you these roses. Seems like a waste of good money to me. But I read somewhere that I'm supposed to do something like this because it's our anniversary. Here—hope you enjoy them."

Would you enjoy such a presentation? I'd throw those babies right in the trash. And yet, that's how many women approach the marriage bed. A man can tell when his wife is participating out of obligation and when she is enjoying loving her man. And even though he may feel some release after the song is sung, he will still feel a void in his heart of hearts.

Let me share one of the secret desires the survey respondents mentioned. Husbands dream of their wives *initiating* sex more often. Notice I said, *more often*. Some of you are trying to remember if you've ever initiated sex, so imagine the joy on his face when you try it the first time.

"But what will he think of me?" you wonder. "Will he think I'm a wanton, sex-crazed woman?" He might hope that's what you are, but he won't think that. He might be utterly confused at your sudden desire, but one message will come across loud and clear. "She wants me! She wants me!" You know what he'll feel. He'll feel like his dreams have come true.

Author and marriage expert Dennis Rainey tells a story about a young seminary student and his wife:

> I will never forget an encounter with the young wife of a seminary student. She came up to me after I had spoken in a class for wives about how they could communicate love to their husbands, and she began to giggle.
>
> "We were driving home the other night from youth group," she said (her husband was a youth pastor). "I turned to him and I said, 'Sweetheart, what would really encourage you to be a man of God?'
>
> There was a moment of silence, and finally he said, 'Well, it would really encourage me if I came home from class one afternoon and found you at home with no clothes on, welcoming me home.'"

The wife giggled again and asked Dennis, "Do you think he really meant it?"

I said, "I don't know. Maybe you ought to try it!"[1]

Now, isn't it interesting that this man who has immersed himself in the study of the Scriptures answered his wife this way? You would think he might want a set of theology books or some time with a great man of God. No, he wants time with his wife, alone, just to be affirmed sexually.

This is a powerful picture. Your husband's sexuality is so much a part of who he is that it affects virtually every part of his life. The wise woman understands that her man longs to be needed sexually by her.

> *What a husband really wants is for his wife to be as excited and enthusiastic about making love as he is.*

If you really want to get to the bottom line for men, and you really want to express love to your husband in a powerful way, just express to your husband that you need him sexually."[2]

Okay, so your husband wants you to want him. Let me tell you what that doesn't mean. It doesn't mean that when he initiates intimacy, you say merely yes and follow along. What I'm talking about here is that your husband wants you to want him before he makes a move. What he really wants is for his wife to be as excited and enthusiastic about making love as he is. He wants to know he's "got what it takes." He's inwardly asking, "Does she really find me desirable?" He's wondering, "Does she really love me?" He's pondering, "Does my wife think I'm hot?"

Author Sheila Wray Gregoire reminds us:

> It's hard for him [your husband] to believe that you're proud of him, and that you're happy to be married to him, if you don't also want him sexually—if you never initiate sex.
>
> If you don't want him like that, then you really don't think he can take on the world. You really don't think he's a capable guy, a strong guy, an amazing guy. You just want to be married to somebody, but you don't actually respect him anymore.
>
> It's men's ultimate self-esteem issue. And the best way to address it is if we, every now and then, actually initiate.[3]

I'm not suggesting that a man wants his wife to initiate sex all the time. That isn't the natural order of things. God created man to be the aggressor and woman to be the recipient. Even our bodies are crafted for such. Men are hunters and women are gatherers. But I can promise you every man likes to feel hunted and captured by the woman of his dreams.

Once you've initiated sex, don't stop there. Be involved! Be an active participant! I don't mean to sound crass, but just lying there and expecting him to do all the "work" says to him that you're just not all that interested.

I wonder how the challenge is going at your house. Here's what Cindy said happened on Day 10 in her home:

> The 14-Day Romance Challenge was the most wonderful, rewarding experience my husband and I have had in the 23 years of our marriage. The first few days he just thanked me for the kind words. When the 3x5 cards, the emails, and texts started showing up, he had a smile that just did not go away. On the eighth day, he asked me what new book I was reading to get all of these ideas from, and on the tenth day he must have told some of his buddies at work, because they wanted him to find out about it so their wives could join the fun.

Romance Challenge Ideas

♥ Make his favorite dessert and eat dinner by candlelight.

♥ Post "I love being your wife!" on his Facebook wall.

♥ Do something fun and unexpected together such as laser tag, horseback riding, bungee cord jumping, rock climbing, or zip lining (I said unexpected!). Or go on a picnic, go to a drive-in movie, take a ballroom dance class, take a boat ride, go to a ball game, or attend a comedy performance.

♥ Make a "wanted" poster like you see in the post office for suspected criminals. Google "wanted poster template." Use a computer editing program such as PicMonkey.com, Photoshop.com, or Pixlr.com and cut and paste his picture on the poster. Or you can print out the poster, print out his picture, and cut and paste his mug on the poster the old-fashioned way. Type onto the poster, "Wanted for excessive hotness. Wanted alive."

♥ Create a romantic setting in a room other than your bedroom. Surprise your husband by leading him into the room for a special rendezvous with you.

Here's What the Guys Said

Our greatest struggle has been in the area of sexual communication and understanding the difference in the importance it is for us individually and as a couple. We have had to learn to make time, to be vulnerable, and to seek each other's needs before our own. We have had to learn each other's "love language" and make adjustments to help meet the other's expectations and needs. The hardest problem is for my wife to understand that my desire for sexual expression is to give and express myself to her.
—Bill

I wish my wife would be more responsive to my sexual

advances and more aggressive in her own advances.
—Dave

Women must understand that men show love by making love. Sexual fulfillment is not a dirty activity done out of duty. —Craig

DAY 11

Remembering What You Need to Remember, Forgetting What You Need to Forget

What do you do when you've lost that lovin' feelin'? Maybe you truly adored your husband in the beginning, but now you can't remember why. Maybe you honestly admired his finer qualities, but now you can't remember what they were. Maybe you appreciated his wonderful attributes, but now you take them for granted. What do you do now?

Starting over may very well be the answer to your marriage problems—as long as it's with the same man!

Here's a statistic you might find interesting. According to an analysis of the National Survey of Families and Households, 86 percent of unhappily married people who stick it out find that, five years later, their marriages are happier. In fact, nearly 60 percent of those who rated their marriage as unhappy and who stayed married rated their same marriage "very happy" or "quite happy" when re-interviewed five years later.[1] In comparison, those who divorced and remarried divorced again at a rate of 60 percent.[2]

Starting over may very well be the answer to your marriage problems—as long as it's with the same man!

In the book of Revelation in the Bible, God had this to say to the church at Ephesus: "I hold this against you: You have forsaken the love you had at first" (Revelation 2:4). Ephesus was one of the most loving churches in the New Testament, and yet somewhere along the way they lost that initial thrill of knowing Christ. Their love for each other and for God had grown cold.

*We can get so busy taking care of life
that we forget to take care of love.*

Perhaps you are a woman who has forgotten the thrill you felt when you first met your husband—the spine-tingling chills when he walked into a room, the heart-skipping flutter when he called on the phone, the tender wooing when you saw his name in your email in-box, the electricity of sexual desire stirred with a kiss. Between taking out the garbage, paying the bills, running the car pool, mowing the lawn, disciplining the kids, and folding the laundry, something got lost. We can get so busy taking care of life that we forget to take care of love.

How do you get that lovin' feelin' back? God gave the

church two simple steps, and I believe we can apply them to marriage as well. "Consider how far you have fallen! Repent and do the things you did at first" (Revelation 2:5).

Remember how it was in the beginning.

Return and do the things you did at first.

Remember what drew you to your husband in the first place? Remember the things you did at first? How you tried to please him, capture his heart, and win his affection? That may have been 50 pounds and a full head of hair ago, but that young man who longed to be adored, admired, and appreciated still lives within his heart. Let him know he does.

Here's what one woman said happened when she took the time to remember and return:

> My husband didn't seem to respond at first except maybe with a smile or thanks. But by the middle of the first week, something fantastic happened— he started romancing me right back! He didn't know what the deal was, or why I had started doing those little things. But he knew it was something he wanted to reciprocate. I think I forgot the reason he was so romantic when we were dating in high school and college was that I did as much of the romancing as he did. It's just something we want to give back when we receive it.

Yes, sometimes we need to remember why we fell in love with our husbands in the first place and return to doing some of the things we did in the early years. At the same time, there are some things we need to forget, or at least forgive and put behind us.

It's difficult to romance your man if you have anger, bitterness, and resentment in your heart. C.S. Lewis said this about forgiveness: "You must make every effort to kill every taste of resentment in your own heart—every wish to humiliate or hurt him or to pay him out. The difference between this situation and the one in which you are asking God's forgiveness is this. In our own case we accept excuses too easily; in other people's we do not accept them easily enough."[3]

He also wrote, "Everyone says forgiveness is a lovely idea until they have something to forgive."[4] I wholeheartedly agree. Forgiveness can be especially difficult when the one who hurt you is the man who promised to love and cherish you all the days of your life. But what is more difficult is to have the marriage of your dreams without forgiveness.

Keeping a record of wrongs is like allowing termites to destroy the foundation of the marriage.

In no way does forgiveness mean turning a blind eye to a problem that needs attention. Pornography, alcoholism, drug abuse, and a plethora of other addictions must be addressed and dealt with for any marriage to survive and thrive. A wife is not doing her husband any favors by allowing such behavior to continue. To ignore such behavior is to enable sin to continue and deposit droplets of poison into a man's soul.

However, keeping a record of wrongs is like allowing termites to destroy the foundation of the marriage.

I recently received an email from a woman who was still bitter over a statement her husband made to her cousin ten years prior. She and her husband were preparing to celebrate their fiftieth wedding anniversary, and she was dreading it because of his careless words a decade ago. She wrote, "Please pray that God mends this *title* piece of my heart that has fallen to the ground."

The word *title* was a typo—she meant to type *little*. To me, it was telling. Friend, we can allow our husband's *little* shortcomings to become the *title* of our story, or we can forgive and start anew.

The first step to forgiveness is prayer. The Bible tells us to pray for our enemies. I hope your husband is never your enemy, but I can assure you, on some days he may feel like it. So let's follow God's instruction and pray for him. Stormie Omartian wrote, "[Prayer] is a gentle tool of restoration appropriated through the prayers of a wife who longs to do right more than be right, and to give life more than to get even."[5] It may not turn your husband's hardened heart to putty in your hands, but it will melt the hardness of resentment in your own.

Paul wrote, "One thing I do: Forgetting what is behind and straining toward what is ahead" (Philippians 3:14). Forgiveness is making a commitment to look ahead and leave the past behind. This requires a refusal to bring up the offense that has already been forgiven. As Sydney J. Harris once said, "There's no point in burying the hatchet if you're going to put up a marker on the site."

Listen to these words from author Lewis Smedes:

> Forgiveness is God's invention for coming to
> terms with a world in which, despite their best
> intentions, people are unfair to each other and
> hurt each other deeply…He [God] began by for-
> giving us. And he invites us all to forgive each
> other. Forgiving is love's toughest work, and love's
> biggest risk…Forgiving seems almost unnatural.
> Our sense of fairness tells us people should pay for
> the wrong they do. But forgiving is love's power to
> break nature's rule…It is forgiving that supplies
> the healing stream of longterm tomorrow.[6]

Forgiveness has little to do with what was done to us and much to do with what we chose to do with it. I believe it is the ultimate expression of love.

On this the eleventh day of the Romance Challenge, let's remember what we need to remember and forget what we need to forget.

Romance Challenge Ideas

♥ Everyone loves a love story. At the dinner table,
tell your kids the story of how you and your husband met. Recall the day your husband asked you
to marry him. I'm sure my son has tired of hearing the story time and time again, but he's never
doubted that his parents are crazy about each other.

♥ Recall a list of firsts: first date, first kiss, first dance, and first time you met each other's parents. Ask your husband what he remembers most about your wedding day and your honeymoon.

♥ Watch a video of your wedding or look at your wedding album together. Talk about what first attracted you to each other.

♥ Pull out photos from your favorite vacations and remember what made them so much fun.

♥ Run your fingers through his hair and give him a head massage. If he doesn't have any hair, a scalp massage will do just fine.

♥ Go back to one of the steamier challenges you skipped and make a new memory. Come on, girl, you can do it.

Here's What the Guys Said

The woman of my dreams is one who is graceful in her demeanor, words, and deeds. She is one who is not judgmental, does not hold a grudge, and does not continue to bring up past mistakes. —Eric

Describe the woman of my dreams? Okay, she needs patience and lots of it! Understanding and love go a long way too. Please forgive me more often...that's really all I ask! —Ron

I wish my wife would kidnap me for a romantic holiday…which we have never done. I'd settle for going to bed earlier so we wouldn't be so tired, and coming to bed with no clothes on! —Zack

I think women need to understand just how critical it is that a husband feels like his wife's hero. —Harry

DAY 12

Serving Love on a Silver Platter

For years I've heard marriage is a 50/50 proposition. But the question is, who gets to decide where the halfway mark is? Dennis Rainey notes, "It is impossible to determine if your spouse has met you halfway because neither of you can agree on where 'halfway' is, each is left to scrutinize the other's performance from his or her own jaded perspective."[1]

Carley and Dan are a couple who have gone the extra mile...not to go the extra mile. They constantly keep score as to who put a new bar of soap in the shower last or who replaced the toilet paper roll last or who opened a new tube of toothpaste last. "It's sort of a contest to see who can use the smallest sliver of soap or use the last drop of toothpaste," Carley boasted. The contest, as silly as it may seem, boils down to who is going to serve the other. Imagine how adored Dan would feel if Carley began to get out a new bar of soap before the sliver war began or replenished the toilet paper before it was totally out.

If you want to try a contest in your home, how about seeing who can out-serve the other! The apostle Paul encourages:

"Don't just pretend to love others. Really love them. Hate what is wrong. Hold tightly to what is good. Love each other with genuine affection and take delight in honoring each other" (Romans 12:9-10 NLT).

> *Whether we are using a telescope to get the big picture or a microscope for close examination, the wife of your man's dreams pays close attention to his needs, desires, dreams, joys, and sorrows.*

When Jesus washed the disciples' feet (John 13:1-17), it wasn't simply an act of kindness. He was actually fulfilling a need the other people had refused to meet. It was customary in those days for the host of a dinner party to have a servant wash the guests' feet. There were no Reeboks or Nikes in those days. Men and women wore leather sandals as they walked the dusty, often muddy, roads of the Holy Land. Nothing felt better than to sink callused, throbbing feet into a cool basin of water and rinse away the cares of the day. However, at Jesus's last supper with His disciples, no servant was available to wash the guests' feet, and no one volunteered.

So God-made-man wrapped a towel around His waist and did what no one else was willing to do. He washed the disciples' feet. Afterward, He sat down and said, "Now that I, your Lord and Teacher, have washed your feet, you also should wash one another's feet. I have set you an example that you should do as I have done for you" (John 13:14-15).

In Philippians 2:4, Paul tells us to look out for the interests of others, not just for our own. "Look out for" is from the Greek word *skopos*, from which we get the words *telescope* and *microscope*. It means to pay close attention. Whether we are using a telescope to get the big picture or a microscope for close examination, the wife of your man's dreams pays close attention to his needs, desires, dreams, joys, and sorrows. She looks closely at his heart and thinks of ways to serve him.

Serving doesn't mean the bondage of slavery. As Jesus put on the towel and served His disciples, He proved to us conclusively that God's kind of serving love flows from choice, not coercion; from strength, not weakness; from gladness, not guilt.

Jesus said, "Give, and it will be given to you. A good measure, pressed down, shaken together and running over, will be poured into your lap. For with the measure you use, it will be measured to you" (Luke 6:38). It may be entirely possible for you to serve your husband and not feel you are receiving anything in return. However, your heavenly Father is always watching, and the measure you use to bless your husband will be used by your heavenly Husband to bless you in return.

Don't be surprised if some of what you're doing starts being reciprocated. Remember, that's not the objective, but sometimes it's a natural consequence. Here's how I saw that happen in a few of the responses:

> Unlike many of the comments you shared in "What the Guys Said," my husband doesn't often initiate intimacy. I usually do. But during the

challenge, to my ABOSOLUTE DELIGHT, that changed. I sent the challenge to girlfriends and it's been great for them too. I've saved each day so I can periodically revisit some.

What fun! I am now starting to get little love notes on my work email when I get in. That has NEVER happened unless he was responding to mine! After 25 years of marriage, a new little spark has emerged!

When I started this challenge, my husband and I were separated after almost a year of struggling with some serious issues. By the half of the challenge he returned home, started marital therapy again, and we even have a trip together for a retreat next week. Praise the Lord!

Romance Challenge Ideas

- ♥ Ask your husband what you can do for him today.

- ♥ Call the radio station he listens to and dedicate a song to him. Ask them to play it when you know he will be in the car (such as on the way to work or on the way home).

- ♥ When he's undressing in the evening, offer to help.

- ♥ When you're out running errands, pick up a little

something you know he'd like. It could be as simple as his favorite candy bar.

♥ Make love and make it all about him. Other than kissing, make it your goal to "serve" him. Let him be completely on the receiving end.

Here's What the Guys Said

My wife discovers what I like and dislike and then anticipates from there. This could come in the form of being the person who writes checks and balances the books, to surprising me with peanut butter chocolates when I'm not looking. —Steve

One thing my wife is really good at is that she doesn't nag, and boy, do I appreciate that! She is not a doormat; she's a tiger and doesn't mind standing her ground with me or anyone if need be. There is a difference between nagging and disagreeing. —Brad

I long to hear my wife tell me some nice, sweet words. —Barumbya

DAY 13

Creating an Atmosphere of Anticipation

I'm sure you already know this, but let me just state it for clarity: Men operate like a light switch—either off or on. However, women are more like a dimmer switch. We start with just a hint of light and then the beam grows as the switch is adjusted. It takes a man just a few seconds to prepare for passion, but it can take a woman several hours to warm up to the idea. I know the ideal situation is for a man to kiss his wife on the cheek in the morning, give her a call in the middle of the day, help load the dishwasher after supper, and then put the kids to bed. That is a woman's ideal idea of foreplay. However, we can't always count on that.

> *Men operate like a light switch—either off or on.*
> *However, women are more like a dimmer switch.*

So what's the solution if your husband doesn't understand that sex begins with a hug in the morning and help around the house in the evening? What do you do when you're more like a Crock-Pot that needs to simmer throughout the day, and your hubby is more like a microwave that goes from chilled to steamy in 60 seconds or less? Perhaps you need to start the Crock-Pot yourself.

Begin the day by thinking about an evening of passion and planning accordingly. Give him a call in the middle of the day. Put a note in his briefcase that makes him want to rush home from the office. As mentioned earlier, maybe you need to mark certain days on your calendar to give your mind a jump-start on the evening. (And can I say right now just how proud I am of you for getting to Day 13!)

You know what I've discovered? I simply told my husband that when he helps me out around the house, it makes me more attracted to him. We're not exchanging favors. I'm not paying him for being "a good boy." It's just the facts. When I feel Steve is loving me by unloading the dishwasher or putting away the laundry (these have become two of his favorite pastimes), it makes me want to eat him up with a spoon! He's figured this out and whistles as he puts those dishes away. But this is about you romancing your man, not him romancing you...just saying.

Stephen Covey, author of *The 7 Habits of Highly Effective People*, wrote that all things are created twice, first mentally and then physically. The key to creativity is to begin with the end in view, with a vision and a blueprint of the desired result.[1] By creating a visual image of making love with your husband, you will be building anticipation in your own mind and taking several steps closer to the desired result.

In their book *Intimate Issues*, Linda Dillow and Lorraine Pintus tell a story about a woman named Heidi. She asked her husband, Brent, what he would like for his birthday present. She expected him to say something ordinary like new golf clubs. Instead, his extraordinary request stunned her: "Honey, the only gift I desire is for you to give yourself permission to be a sensuous woman." Heidi's eyes filled with tears.[2]

> *Sexual fulfillment between a husband and wife is not only the dream of your man; it is the design of a holy God.*

One thing that was so precious to me as I read the responses from the men who completed my surveys and interviews when I was writing *Becoming the Woman of His Dreams* is that they loved their wives and really wanted great marriages. The woman of their dreams is a combination of deeply spiritual and divinely sexual. Those two are not separate entities. They are one and the same, and I've come to realize that men have a better handle on that than most of us women. Sexual fulfillment between a husband and wife is not only the dream of your man; it is the design of a holy God.

Here's what a couple of women who finished the challenge said about what they discovered:

> This has been a lot of fun! It also helped me to see more clearly the needs of my husband and how important it is to him to feel special. The guys

at work at first teased him over the little valentine cards in his lunch box and the candy lips and kisses. But by the time the 14-Day Challenge was over, one guy said, "Your wife makes you lunch and gives you valentines! Mine just says here's some money, buy your own!"

My husband is deployed, so I was unable to utilize most of the little things we could do each day. I did, however, send him a Valentine's Day package. It had his favorite nuts, candy, and a list of 50 things I love, admire, and respect most about him. I told him I could have easily come up with another 100, but since he turned 50 last month, I decided to keep to the "50" theme. He said the list made him laugh and cry. He also said he has never felt so loved by anyone in his life...EVER. He was so grateful and said it made him want to be an even better man.

Romance Challenge Ideas

♥ Purchase a blank puzzle at a craft store. Write a romantic message on the puzzle. Break it up in pieces, place it in a box, and give it to your husband as a little love gift.

♥ Buy some temporary tattoos and tattoo each other in a place only the two of you will see.

♥ Serve up some chocolate-covered strawberries as a snack for two.

♥ Purchase an inexpensive box of kid's valentine cards and leave a trail throughout his day—in his underwear drawer, in his sock drawer, on his shoes, on his cereal box, on his car seat, in his lunch bag, in his briefcase, and so on. Put the last one on his pillow as a special invitation.

♥ Put the pillows at the foot of the bed to mix it up a bit. You might be surprised what happens when you remove the routine and the expected.

Here's What the Guys Said

The woman of my dreams is sold-out for God. She is a spiritual and a sexual person—a prayer partner and a sexual partner. —Kevin

My wife is the woman of my dreams. I know that she loves and respects me. Our greatest struggle has been our sex life. I wish she understood that I need to be needed in a physical way. I don't want her to view the physical aspect of our life as a chore or an obligation that she has as a wife, but something she looks forward to as a woman. Her innocence as a teenager and young woman attracted me, but as the years go by, I guess I long to see her grow into a woman who is not embarrassed by her needs. —Al

In a world where there is so much temptation facing men, I think it's important for wives to know when to stop being "wife and mom" and start being a "lover." —Buck

DAY 14

Responding to Him

Can you believe we're on our last day of the Romance Challenge? I'd love to see the look on your husband's face today! I'm thinking Cheshire Cattish. Let's move into the last day and tie it up with a bow.

Do you want to know what your man desires more than anything? This may surprise you, but he wants to see *you* sexually fulfilled. He longs for you to respond to him. He wants to know he is the one who can take you to the moon and back with a crescendo of ecstasy *he* created.

> *Most men want to be their wives' heroes.*

He longs to know he is a great lover. As Dr. Kevin Leman states, "There is not a man on the planet who doesn't want to know he can make his woman go crazy in bed."[1] Leman also says, "Even more than your husband wants to have sex with you for his own sexual relief, the truth is, he wants to please you even more than he wants to be pleased. It might seem like it's all about him, but what he really wants, emotionally,

113

is to see how much you enjoy the pleasure he can give you. If he fails to do that, for any reason, he'll end up feeling inadequate, lonely, and unfulfilled. Most men want to be their wives' heroes."[2]

A husband is looking for fulfillment, not accommodation. Simply put, he is sexually fulfilled when his wife is fulfilled. If he knows she is not enjoying sex, but only trying to placate him, he will not be fulfilled or satisfied. Sex may happen, he may finish what was begun, but he will have unfinished business in his heart. He will feel like a consumer, not a lover.

I want you and your husband to try an experiment. Find a piano bench and sit side by side before the ivory keys. Once you get comfortable, place both your hands on the keys and play a melodious duet, complete with highs and lows, rises and falls, sharps and flats.

What? You say that's ridiculous? You don't know how to play the piano? Well, why not? You have fingers. The piano has keys. It should come naturally, shouldn't it?

Very few people are born with the natural ability to play a piano "by ear." The vast majority have to study the art and spend hours of practice before they can run their fingers over the keys to produce a beautiful melody. Some learn enough just to play "Chopsticks" and others progress to "Beethoven's Fifth."

Likewise, for most people great sex does not come naturally. It takes practice and maybe even a little study. Several great books on sexual intimacy from a Christian perspective are available. In this book I have quoted from four of my favorites: *Intimate Issues* by Linda Dillow and Lorraine Pintus,

Sheet Music by Dr. Kevin Leman, *Intended for Pleasure* by Dr. Ed and Gaye Wheat, and *Red-Hot Monogamy* by Bill and Pam Farrel.

Romance is certainly about more than what happens in the bedroom, but in your husband's book, it is very important. I hope you've gleaned some great ideas to help you let your husband know just how much you adore, admire, and appreciate him! I hope you've romanced his socks off!

As the challenge comes to a close, think about the ways you've seen a change in your marriage. Was it fun? I hope so.

Here's what a couple more women had to say about what they saw happen in their home.

> Such a great experience. I ended the 14 days with a trail of children's valentines around the house where my husband would find them. One on the lid of the toilet seat, one on his shaving mirror, one in his underwear drawer, one in his Bible, one on his steering wheel, etc. He enjoyed the "scavenger hunt" to find them and said, "I have the best wife in the world! I'm telling Facebook!"

> Thank you for motivating me to amp up the romance. I was amazed at how quickly I saw my husband thrive on the attention I was giving him. These last two weeks have been awesome and I certainly plan to continue to keep our marriage flavored with sugar and spice! I'm married to an amazing man who puts our small children and

me first each and every day. AND he's hot! Thank you for giving me new inspiration to show him appreciation and for reminding me of the kind of wife my heavenly Father designed me to be!

Romance Challenge Ideas

♥ Have romantic music playing when he comes home from work or gets out of the shower.

♥ Flirt with him at the dinner table. Run your foot up his leg. Place your hand on his thigh.

♥ Put a love note or a special invitation on the windshield of his car while he's at work or before he gets into the car in the morning.

♥ If he takes a shower at night, hide all his underwear.

♥ Get him an engraved trophy that says, "World's Best Husband." Trophy shops will engrave anything you'd like. I got one for my husband after he coached me through the birth of our son that said, "Coach of the Year."

♥ Go back over the previous challenges and tackle one of the steamier ideas as the grand finale of your 14-day journey! And remember…it doesn't have to stop here!

Here's What the Guys Said

I wish my wife understood my need to make time for intimacy a priority. Otherwise, she is a perfect wife!
—Allen

The woman of my dreams is one that is interested in sexually pleasing her husband by finding out what turns him on and exploring their sexuality together. —Eric

The woman of my dreams lets me know that she appreciates what I do for her and the family. —Dave

My wife is the woman of my dreams in every way.
—Bob

Congratulations!

C ongratulations on completing the 14-Day Romance Challenge! I am so proud of you.

I know you can't keep up this pace every day, but I encourage you to set aside certain times during the year to lavish your hubby with concentrated times of romance. Sprinkle romantic gestures in his days when he least expects it.

I'd love to hear what happened during the challenge. I've created a website comment page for you to share how the challenge affected your marriage and your man. I'll let you keep the intimate details tucked away in your heart, but I'd love to hear about your husband's reaction, the change you saw in your marriage, and what transpired in your own heart.

So please, visit this webpage and share away! Simply type the following in your search bar browser: www.sharonjaynes.com/romance.

Let's celebrate together!

150 Additional Ways to Romance Your Husband

I hope you enjoyed the ideas for romancing your husband in the 14-Day Romance Challenge, but I'm thinking…why stop now! Here is a list of some additional ways to romance your man over the days, weeks, and years to come. But before you begin, keep this in mind:

Every man is different. What says love to one man will not necessarily say love to another. Is your husband a man who loves nothing more than having a good book in one hand and his favorite beverage in the other? Or is he a rod-and-reel sort of guy who loves nothing more than spending a day outdoors? Is he a meat-and-potato sort of guy or quinoa, kale, and sushi sort? Pay attention to what says love to your man and choose the ideas that will mean the most to him.

Romance to your husband might be watching ESPN, eating tacos on a tray table, followed by some fun under the sheets with you. Another husband's idea of romance is soft music, a candlelit room, and of course, being under the sheets with you. You might want to ask your husband to describe what lets him know you love him or what is romantic to him.

Most likely you've seen what makes his heart sing from the ideas you tried in the challenge.

Peruse the following ideas to pick and choose what you think would let your husband know you're crazy about him and give them a try. Also, I encourage you to try an idea that you're not quite sure about. One that might even make you a little uncomfortable. It's okay! That's what stretching and growing is all about. You might be surprised at his response and learn something new about that man you married.

Put a check mark by the ideas you would like to try. Then draw a heart around the ones he loved.

1. Hang a piece of lingerie among his shirts. Pin a note to it that says, "Let me know when you find this and I'll try it on for you."

2. Hide a tiny piece of lingerie in his coat pocket with a note that says, "I'm thinking of you today."

3. Hide a love note in his wallet among the bills with a note that says, "You are worth more to me than all the money in the world."

4. Hide a tiny piece of lingerie in his gym bag. If it happens to fall out at the gym, the other guys will simply think he is the luckiest man on the planet.

5. Tell your husband he looks handsome in front of other people. One of my friends commented on her husband's appearance, "Doesn't that shirt Pat has on make his eyes look so blue! He's

so handsome." Pat blushed a little, but he also grinned a lot.

6. Make your husband a coupon booklet for some of his favorite things. I'll let you come up with the ideas. Remember, think of his love language. It doesn't need to be all sexual ideas. It could be a coupon for making his favorite dessert. One friend asked her husband what she could do to show him how much she loved him and he said, "Fix me a fruit salad." Who knew?

7. When you're out to dinner, write a note on a paper napkin telling him you are looking forward to dessert when you get home. And I'm not talking about a fruit salad.

8. When you're out to dinner, write "I love you" on a paper napkin.

9. Google how to give a massage and then practice on each other.

10. Let him enjoy his favorite hobby guilt free.

11. Go camping in your backyard. Pitch a tent, have a picnic, and then smooch under the stars.

12. Show interest in his work by asking good questions. "What is the most interesting thing that happened at work today?" "What was the most frustrating thing that happened at work

today?" "What is the best thing that happened today?"

13. Go to the mall together and let him pick out a new fragrance for you, and you pick out a new fragrance for him. Then let those fragrances be for your "special" times together. They can also serve as a signal that you're in the mood. If you're on a budget, ask the sales person for several samples.

14. After making love, tell him how wonderful it was...how amazing he is. Tell him you are so lucky to have such a wonderful lover for a husband.

15. Put on a non-see-through bathrobe, made of material such as flannel or terry cloth, with nothing underneath. You can even have this on while the kids are still up. But then in a moment when no one is around, quickly flash him and wink.

16. Order his favorite takeout and have it delivered to his office. Have the restaurant write a note on the box that says, "From your biggest fan."

17. Admire his muscles, give them a little squeeze, and tell him you appreciate the way he takes care of himself.

18. Give him a massage from head to toe. Use lotion or massaging oils to enhance the experience.

19. Brag about him to a family member and make sure he overhears it.

20. Purchase something for him that he's always wanted. Pay attention. While a woman's favorite gifts might not have a plug or a motor, your husband's might.

21. Praise him in front of the kids. "You'll never believe what your dad did today. He…"

22. When you and he have the house to yourself, leave rose petals or articles of clothing from the door to the bedroom. For an extra touch, have lit candles to light the way.

23. Write an invitation for lovemaking on a steamed-up mirror when your husband is in the shower and be waiting in your candlelit bedroom.

24. Write him a love note or purchase a greeting card and mail it to his office.

25. If he cooks his own eggs in the morning, draw on each egg, "I ♥ U" or your initials + his initials.

26. If he eats cereal in the morning, write "Gift Inside" on the outside of the cereal box with a marker. Then put a little something in the box that will make him smile. Think about what manufacturers usually put in food boxes as a treat for a child and then customize it for your man: a ChapStick, an "I love you" sticker, a mini

flashlight, a kid's valentine card, a little candle, and so on.

27. When he doesn't expect it, on an ordinary day, let him notice that you have on sexy unmentionables when you're undressing to go to bed. Don't make a big deal about it. Let him just happen to see it.

28. Put his head in your lap and run your fingers through his hair or rub his head while he's watching television.

29. Caress his face when you kiss him.

30. Go back to the place you had your first date and remember when.

31. Recreate the moment when your husband asked you to marry him. Only this time, you do the asking. You don't have to get on one knee, but you could have a romantic speech prepared. Rather than offering an engagement ring, do something else fun, such as offering him a rose to pin on his shirt and ask, "Will you accept this rose?"

32. Plan a second honeymoon to the place where you experienced your first.

33. If you share a favorite line from a poem or a song, display it in your home. For example, stencil the phrase on a wall, print it off in a beautiful font and place it in a frame, or have it engraved on a metal frame and place a picture of the two of you

in it. My husband had a plaque made with a line from one of our favorite songs burned into the wood. Okay, you want to know what it says, don't you? It says "Paradise...population two."

34. Get a Scrabble board and use the letters to spell out your favorite memories together. I ordered extra letters online, hot glued the letters spelling out some of our favorite places and memories onto the board, and then mounted it in a shadowbox frame. (It can take a lot of finagling to get the words to connect. Don't glue the letters to the board until you get all the letters exactly where you want them.)

35. Cook dinner in an apron only. (For some husbands, it might be romantic for their wives to cook dinner period.)

36. Write out your love story and have it bound. You can find several options for this online.

37. Purchase a package of children's valentine cards and use them throughout the year.

38. Make a list of his best qualities from A to Z and give it to him.

39. Wash his hair.

40. Light candles at dinner.

41. Play music in the bedroom.

42. Create a romantic playlist for his iPod.

43. Tell him you're glad you married him.

44. Place your hand on his leg when sitting beside him in the car.

45. Go to a playground and swing.

46. Walk on a beach.

47. Do a service project together, such as building a Habitat for Humanity home or tutoring underprivileged kids. Yes, that is romantic and creates endorphins.

48. Turn off all electronics for one night.

49. Leave a note on his pillow that says "Room service" with a list of options.

50. Determine to have a ten-second hug every day when he comes home from work or when you both get home from work. When we started doing this, I was amazed at how much longer the ten-second hug was than our usual hug had been.

51. Place heart stickers in unexpected places: his underwear drawer, his toolbox, on the remote control, or on his toothpaste tube.

52. In cold weather, clean off his windshield and warm up the engine.

53. Download and email him a love song.

54. Place a bowl of small, heart-shaped candies in your bedroom. Place one heart on his pillow as a

sign that tonight is the night. Invite him to send you the same signal as well.

55. Purchase a red dinner plate and write "I love you today and always" around the rim. You can use a paint marker, a washable marker, or even icing.

56. If your husband travels, leave him a message at the front desk of the hotel where he's staying.

57. Put an "I ♥ my husband" bumper sticker on your car. (I have these available at SharonJaynes.com.)

58. Send him a series of thank-you notes to his workplace. You could send one per day for 14 days or one per week for 14 weeks. Of course, it doesn't have to be 14. You choose. Thank him for things such as the way he takes care of your family, the way he reflects Christ, the way he shows you he loves you, for paying the bills, for taking care of the lawn, for being a great father, for being kind to your parents. Thank him for one thing in each card. As the cards add up, his love tank will fill up.

59. Tell him you love him before you hang up the phone…every time.

60. Come up with a secret sign to let him know you love him.

61. Pat his bottom when he walks by you in the house.

62. Leave a sweet voicemail on his phone.

63. Text him to let him know you're thinking about him.

64. Take him breakfast in bed.

65. Take him coffee while he's shaving.

66. Celebrate little victories: winning a race, making a sale, closing a case, or finishing a project.

67. Post a picture of him on Facebook with a hashtag such as #hothubby or #bestdad and make sure to tag him.

68. Read a book your husband has enjoyed, and then ask him to go out to coffee and discuss it together.

69. Burn a CD of favorite love songs and put it in his car with a love note: "As you listen to these songs, remember how much I love you."

70. Kiss him when he comes in the door in the evening.

71. Kiss him before he leaves for work in the morning.

72. Perhaps #71 was a quick kiss. Now try this. Give him a passionate kiss before he leaves for work in the morning. I mean one he will remember for the rest of the day.

73. Fold his T-shirts and pair his socks the way he likes them, even if you think it's silly and not important.

74. Write a pretend newspaper article about the

world's most amazing husband. At the top
write: News Flash! The World's Most Amazing
Husband Discovered on (your street address).
Print it out on the computer and place it in the
pages of the newspaper before he reads it.

75. Thank him for changing the oil in your car,
cutting the grass, or any other task you may have
taken for granted or simply thought of as his duty
as a husband. Let him know you appreciate how
he takes care of you and your family.

76. Frame a picture of your husband (just him, not
with kids or anyone else) and put it in a place
where he knows you look often. That tells him
you enjoy looking at him and thinking about him
throughout the day.

77. Send him a text that says, "I'm thinking about
you today."

78. Have your husband write down ten of his favorite
things, one on each of ten slips of paper. Put them
in a bowl or jar and let him pick one for you to do
together. Continue over several weeks until you've
done them all.

79. If he has a favorite Starbucks coffee, purchase the
equipment and learn how to make it yourself.
If he likes a certain flavor, such as gingerbread,
peppermint, or brown sugar maple, you can order
the flavorings online from various vendors. If

he likes a latte, you can purchase an inexpensive handheld milk frother as well.

80. If he loves Starbucks, surprise him at the office with a cup of his favorite brew.

81. Duplicate your husband's favorite restaurant meal in your own kitchen. Go to www.copykat.com, a site dedicated to providing recipes from your favorite restaurants. Food from the Cheesecake Factory, Longhorn Steakhouse, Carrabba's Italian Grill, and Cracker Barrel are just a few of the restaurant menu items included.

82. Tell him he's the reason for the smile on your face.

83. Wear a fragrance he likes. My husband likes Midnight Pomegranate body lotion from Bath and Body Works. When they discontinued it, I stocked up with enough for several years. For your husband, it might be a perfume, a lotion, or a body spritz.

84. Give the sheets a spritz with a scent he loves. There are spritzes specifically made for sheets. You can also use a body spritz for a yummy clean scent.

85. Make a video on your phone of you telling your husband why you love him. Send it to him as a text message or email. This will be something I bet he won't erase but play again and again.

86. Find five things he does well and tell him about

them. Be specific. For example: "You are a great friend to Tom." "You are so kind to my mom." "You really know how to make our daughter feel special." "You are such a hard worker."

87. Take a picture of your husband doing something you appreciate or admire and then post it on social media. Make sure to tag him so he will see it. For example: Take a picture of him helping your child with something such as brushing his or her teeth with text that says, "What a great dad!" Take a picture of him working in the yard with text that says, "Check out this hot sweaty hunky man! I'm the luckiest girl alive."

88. To piggy back suggestion #87, text those pictures to your husband's cell phone with a message.

89. De-clutter your bedroom. Don't allow it to be a catch-all for laundry that needs folding, bills that need paying, or newspapers that need tossing. Make your bedroom the most beautiful room in the house so it's relaxing, refreshing, and rejuvenating. If your bedroom has not been very inviting in the past, let your husband know you want it to be a special place where you can both escape. See 14 Tips to a More Romantic Bedroom on page 151.

90. If your children are grown, tell him what qualities

you see in them that are reflections of his great parenting.

91. Write "I love my husband" or "(your name) loves (your husband's name)" on your sidewalk or driveway with colored chalk.

92. Find your husband's car at his workplace. With chalk write "I love you" and sign your name on the parking lot surface so he will see it when he gets in the car.

93. String clear Christmas lights around the four posts of your bed or from post to post.

94. Give him 12 days of Christmas he'll never forget. Write him a note and tell him his present will be arriving early this year. Then plan something romantic for December 1 through December 12. Who knows, "The Twelve Days of Christmas" might become his favorite holiday song.

95. Place a lipstick kiss on his car's rearview mirror.

96. Write him a traditional thank-you note and mail it to his office. Thank him for something he did that meant a lot to you or for some specific ways he is a good husband.

97. Wear a piece of jewelry he has given you in the past…and perhaps nothing else.

98. Purchase undies for yourself that you know he will like.

99. Turn down the sheets in a beautiful way and perhaps sprinkle some rose petals to let him know the bed is ready for love. You can purchase one rose at the grocery store for the occasion.

100. Hire someone to mow the lawn on his regular yard workday. Write him a note that says, "I didn't want you to be tired tonight." Draw a smiley face or a heart.

101. Give him a compliment every day. Come up with a system to remember, such as putting a sticker on your bathroom mirror and then removing it once you've given your compliment.

102. Place an "I love you" message in the "personals" column of your local newspaper. Send him an email or text alerting him to read the personals on the day it appears.

103. Come up with a sign to let your husband know tonight is the night. One older woman told me her husband said he would put a dollar in a jar every time they made love. The dollars were their savings for a future cruise. Their signal was that one of them would slyly say, "I've got a dollar in my pocket." How cute is that! By the way, they've taken several cruises.

104. Make a slide show on your computer of your favorite pictures. You can even set it to music. Many computers have this program readily

available. You can go to YouTube for tutorials on how to create them.

105. Carve I ♥ U in a pumpkin in the fall or a watermelon in the summer.

106. Make a scrapbook filled with pictures of your favorite memories. You can also include ticket stubs to ball games or plays. Whatever brings back the memory for you. Then sit down together and relive some of your favorite moments. Don't make this about the kids, but about the two of you.

107. Order custom-made M&Ms and give them to him as a surprise. Do an internet search to find an online company or go to www.mymms.com. You can put images, text, clip art, or even your faces on them. What fun!

108. Tie an "I love you message" to your pet's collar so your husband will have to take it off to read it.

109. Put a love note in the pages of a book or magazine he's reading. When he gets to that page, he will be surprised and reminded of what a great wife he has.

110. Bake an "I love you" message inside a pastry or slip it inside a fortune cookie. Imagine his surprise when he sees the message from his girl!

111. Put an "I love you" message in his favorite bag of chips or box of cereal. Make sure this is his personal stash so the kids don't get it.

112. Write him a love letter. If you are unsure how to start, see 10 Easy Steps to Writing a Love Letter on page 161.

113. Ask him what he enjoys most during lovemaking. Don't be afraid to try something new.

114. Feed each other a yummy dessert.

115. Take a candlelit bubble bath together and sip on your favorite beverage.

116. Write a love note on a roll of paper towels he uses. Don't put it on the first sheet that shows, but on a second one so that he will be surprised when he unrolls and removes the top sheet.

117. Put a helium balloon in his car with the words "I love you" on it.

118. Make a banner that says "I love you" and put it on the ceiling over your bed.

119. Write a love note on a large cookie or cake with icing.

120. Put a temporary tattoo on your body and ask him to find it.

121. Purchase chocolate body paint or get creative with a can of whipped cream.

122. After you go to bed and the lights are out, and it is obvious that tonight is not the night, light a candle, reach over, stir your husband, and say,

"You aren't really sleepy, are you?" I bet he'll say, "No, ma'am."

123. Create a spa night for your husband. Print out a card with a list of services you provide and let him pick.

124. Celebrate his half birthday, letting him know that one day of the year is simply not enough to celebrate the wonder of who he is!

125. If he travels, slip a love note or a card into his suitcase.

126. Tell him that a particular day is going to be a "Yes, dear" day when his every request will be met by you.

127. Create a love note by cutting out words from a magazine and pasting them onto a sheet of paper like a ransom note.

128. Play Twister.

129. Take a hot air balloon ride.

130. Renew your wedding vows. If you can't find a copy of the exact vows you said when you were first married, write new ones.

131. Find an old lantern that resembles a genie lantern. Tell your husband you are going to grant him three wishes under $100. I suspect at least one might not cost you a dime.

132. Find the most romantic place in your hometown and watch the sunset.

133. Put love notes in plastic Easter eggs. Hide them and tell him he has to find them.

134. Whisper in his ear just how much you enjoyed your recent lovemaking.

135. Write a love message on your husband's back with your fingernail. Ask him if he can figure out what you wrote. You might need to go one letter at a time.

136. When your husband goes out to play a competitive sport, put a note in his gym bag, golf bag, or tennis racket cover that says, "I'm cheering for you today."

137. Place a chalkboard somewhere in your house and write love notes to him on it. Many gifts shops and craft stores have trendy chalkboards to fit right in with your décor.

138. Make a paper chain of 25 of his best qualities. Hang it from the door of your bedroom or bathroom. Tell him he can tear off one per day for the next 25 days. Make the last one a doozie.

139. Use magnetic letters or magnetic words to leave messages on your refrigerator door letting your husband (and the world) know how much you love him. You can also have custom words created at various online sites.

140. Go dancing. My husband and I love to dance, and it all started on our first date. That's a story for another time.

141. If you and your husband aren't dancers, consider taking a dance class at a community center or a ballroom dance studio together. Learning how to move as one and following his lead is very romantic…even if you do step on each other's toes from time to time. Plus it's a reason to spend more time together doing something fun. If this is something he's hesitant to try, suggest he give you dance lessons as a Christmas present. It might be a way to ease him into trying it. Once he does, he'll love it. If he tries it and doesn't like it, don't push. But it's worth a try.

142. Set up a candlelight dinner in a room of your house other than the kitchen or breakfast room— in front of a fire in the family room or in the backyard surrounded by tiki torches.

143. Challenge your husband to a game of strip checkers. Every time one player jumps and takes the other player's checker, off comes a piece of clothing.

144. Send him a text, an email, or put a sticky note on his bathroom mirror that says, "Yes." If or when he asks you what it means, wink and tell him, "Whatever you want it to mean."

145. Kiss every time you see something specific. My friends Bill and Pam Farrel kiss after saying grace before a meal. You can kiss every time you see a black cow, a red bird, a cat, and so on. It can be silly and fun.

146. Purchase a pack of sticky notes and keep them intact. Right a love note on each sheet and put the entire pack in his desk drawer, briefcase, or by the remote.

147. When reading fortune cookies at a restaurant, add "under the sheets" to the fortune. It might read something like this: You will have an important meeting today...under the sheets. You will find approval today...under the sheets. Something unusual is going to happen to you today...under the sheets.

148. Purchase blue ribbon (the type that someone would get for winning first prize) and tape it to his bathroom mirror or to his steering wheel, or tuck inside his lunch box or briefcase. Write a note that says, "You have first place in my heart." You can find first-place ribbons at craft shops, discount stores, or online.

149. Make a dinner full of love: heart-shaped hamburger patties or meatloaf with catsup topping, pink mashed potatoes, red congealed salad, strawberries with whipped cream,

heart-shaped bread, red velvet cake, and the like. Tell him you were thinking of him when you were cooking dinner and you just couldn't help yourself. This was the result!

150. Send him on a treasure hunt where one clue leads to the next. Let the last clue lead him to you waiting for him dressed in sexy lingerie. Use sticky notes for the clues.

Here's an example of a first clue: "You have been invited on a treasure hunt. Follow the clues to win your prize. The first clue is found where you go when you're thirsty" (on the refrigerator). Second clue: "The second clue is found where you go for wisdom" (on his Bible). Third clue: "The third clue is found where you wash your clothes" (the washing machine). You get the idea. Write as many clues as you want, but the last one should lead to your bedroom. Tie a blue ribbon around your waist that says, "You win! Here's your prize!"

10 Ways to Romance Your Husband According to His Love Language

In Day 4 of the 14-Day Romance Challenge, I encouraged you to learn your husband's love language. Below are ten simple ways to romance your man according to his particular love language.

Words of Affirmation

1. Tell or write a note to your husband, listing five reasons you're proud to be his wife.

2. Tell or write a note to your husband, listing five reasons you're glad you married him.

3. Tell or write a note to your husband, listing five ways he's an inspiration to others.

4. Tell or write a note to your husband, listing five ways he's a reflection of Christ.

5. Tell or write a note to your husband, listing five reasons he's a great lover.

6. When you see him do something as simple as picking up a piece of trash in public, returning a stray shopping buggy, or being kind to a cashier, let him know you are proud of him for being such a great guy.

7. To piggyback on #6, when you get home, tell your kids what their dad did in front of him. Perhaps at the dinner table, go into detail about when their dad paid for someone's gas at the pump, when he complimented a receptionist and made her smile, or when he opened the door for an older woman at Walmart.

8. When he checks the locks before going to bed, fills up your car with gas, or calls to make sure you reached your destination, tell him you appreciate how he makes you feel safe and cared for.

9. When you catch him being a great dad, let him know about it.

10. Tell your husband what you love about his physic…he'll eat it up. "I love the way your arm muscles bulge when you pick up something heavy." "I love the way your legs look after you've gone for a run." "I love the way your tush looks in those jeans."

Quality Time

1. Ask your husband out on a date and make all the arrangements.

2. Plan a day together. Go out to breakfast. Take a walk. Go to a sports game, art exhibit, or Home Depot. Go to a movie.

3. Snuggle up to your husband while he watches his favorite sports game. Let him make comments about the game (even if you have no idea what he's talking about). When he says, "Watch this replay," watch it. Oh girl, big points.

4. Plan a night away from the kids, the chores, the TV, the computer, and the to-do lists. Tell him you want him all to yourself for just a few hours.

5. Surprise him by arranging for one of his friends to fly or drive in for a special occasion such as his birthday.

6. Ask your husband to teach you to play a game or activity he enjoys, such as tennis, golf, Frisbee, in-line skating, running, archery, or riflery.

7. Find some games just the two of you can play, such as Gin Rummy, Scrabble, or Cornhole.

8. Cook a meal together.

9. Ride along with him when he runs errands.

10. Have an in-home date night with a bowl of his favorite snack and a movie.

Receiving Gifts

1. Grab him a little goody from the grocery store the next time you go. Let him know it was just for him. It could be something as small as his favorite candy bar. Make sure the kids know the goody is just for Dad.

2. Purchase him a gift card for a car wash.

3. If he's a reader, set up an Amazon alert to let you know when his favorite author has a new book out. Purchase it before he even knows about the release.

4. Did your husband have a favorite television series when he was younger? Check to see if it's available online and purchase it for him. My husband loved the old *Mission Impossible* series from the '70s. He was thrilled when I found the DVDs for five seasons online.

5. Pay attention to gadgets that would make his life easier and surprise him with one on an ordinary day—not his birthday. Is his Weed Eater falling apart? Do his work gloves have holes? Has he complained that his electric razor blades are dull? Pay attention and give him a sweet surprise that lets him know you're listening.

6. Purchase a gift that ties in with his favorite hobby. A box of high quality golf balls for the golfer. A special pair of socks for the runner. A can of

top-notch balls for the tennis player. If you aren't sure what would be a great gift for his hobby, ask one of his friends who shares that hobby. I often ask Steve's golf buddy and prayer partner. Chip always has great ideas for golf goodies I never even knew existed.

7. When you're out shopping for new clothes, pick up a shirt or tie for him you think he might like.

8. Surprise him with a ticket to a sports game. You might want to purchase two so he can take a friend along.

9. Save up throughout the year and buy him an extravagant Christmas or birthday gift— something he would never buy for himself.

10. If your husband has a favorite author, purchase a copy of one of his or her books, send it to the author, and ask for an autograph addressed to your husband inside. You might be surprised how readily authors will do that for you. Make sure to include a return postage envelope. The easier you make it for the author, the more likely he or she will follow through.

Acts of Service

1. Clean out the inside of his car and leave a note that says, "Cleaned with hands of love."

2. Carefully wash his favorite grungy baseball hat.

3. Ask him what he would like for dinner and then cook it.

4. Polish his favorite shoes.

5. If he takes his shirts to the cleaners, pick them up for him without him asking.

6. If he's a coffee drinker, have coffee brewing in the mornings or after dinner. Know how he likes it and have it ready.

7. Make him his favorite dessert for no special reason.

8. Ask him if there's an errand you can do for him today.

9. Replace his tattered underwear and worn out socks. Make sure to purchase the very same brand and style he already has. That way you know you're getting something he likes. Men are pretty picky about their undies and socks. If you buy a different brand or style, he won't see it as helping.

10. Fill up the propane tank for the gas grill so when it's time to barbecue he's all ready.

Physical Touch

1. Hold his hand when you're walking side by side… every time.

2. Pat his back or bottom when he walks through the room.

3. Give him quick pecks on the cheek often.

4. Stop what you're doing when he comes home from work and give him a ten-second hug. You'll be surprised how long ten seconds is. Tell him the ten-second rule is a new rule that you have to obey every day. That's one rule he'll love. It often makes my husband and me laugh.

5. Give him a back rub after a hard day.

6. Hold his face in your hands when you kiss him.

7. Place your hand on his thigh or give his thigh a squeeze when you're sitting side by side.

8. Rub his arm when you're sitting beside him on the couch.

9. Place your hand on his arm or hand when he's talking to you.

10. Stroke his hair (or head).

14 Tips for a More Romantic Bedroom

Now that you have gone through the 14-Day Romance Challenge or are in the middle of the challenge, here's another challenge for you...make your bedroom the most romantic room in the house. I double dare you.

If you're like most people, it is easy for the master bedroom to become the catchall for things undone and chores to do—not exactly an invitation to romance. Unfortunately, the one room in the house that should be a haven for intimacy—the bedroom—often becomes a cumulative collection of clutter: a place to dump laundry that needs to be folded, pile up bills that need to be paid, stash magazines you're planning to read, store kids' art projects that need to be filed, or toss items you don't want unexpected guests to see. And, friend, it is difficult to feel romantic and sexy in a room filled with clutter. It reeks of busyness, disorganization, and chores that loom low.

Your bedroom should be a place to escape from the hectic pace of everyday life and reconnect with your husband verbally, emotionally, and physically. Let's look at 14 ideas to reclaim your bedroom and make it the most inviting and romantic room in your house.

1. Make your bed every morning.

It take less than two minutes to make your bed. This one simple act makes the entire room appear more organized and inviting. Think of how you feel when you walk into a hotel room and see a nicely made bed. It makes you excited about pulling back the covers and snuggling in fresh sheets.

An additional bonus in making your bed is that it gives you a sense of accomplishment! If you accomplish nothing else for the day, at least you've made your bed.

I just had to smile when I read the 2014 commencement speech from the University of Texas by U.S. Navy Admiral William H. McRaven: "If you make your bed every morning, you will have accomplished the first task of the day. It will give you a small sense of pride, and it will encourage you to do another task, and another, and another. By the end of the day that one task completed will have turned into many tasks completed...If you want to change the world, start off by making your bed."[1]

2. De-clutter the love nest.

Pick up everything that doesn't belong on the floor and put it in one of three piles: put away, give away, and throw away. Everything besides furniture, lamps, plants, and baskets will most likely go into one of those three piles. Now deal with them.

Put dirty clothes in the clothes hamper.

Throw the trash away and don't look back.

Put those items to donate in a give-away bag you can't see

through, put it in your car for drop-off at the Salvation Army or Goodwill, and don't look back.

Then put the other items where they need to live: bills in a basket on a desk, receipts in a file or envelope in a drawer, buttons in a button jar in a closet, keys in a pretty dish on the dresser or on a hanger by the back door, and children's schoolwork in an expandable folder or plastic tub stored in their rooms, perhaps under their beds. (Extra tip: At the end of the school year, go back through the tubs, save what you'd like to keep, and toss the rest.)

Take a look at what you have on the surfaces of your nightstands, side tables, chests, and dressers. Is anything on them unattractive? Get rid of it.

Does anything remind you of chores to be done or bills to be paid? Move it to a file in another part of the house.

Are there books you are planning to read but haven't gotten around to yet? Place them on a bookshelf in your family room or study.

Do you see loose change on the dresser? Put it in a dish in a top drawer to keep it out of sight.

Are large items such as blankets you aren't using or out-of-season clothes you aren't wearing piled up? Store them in plastic tubs and place them under your bed.

Place only beautiful and inviting items on surfaces in your bedroom. If anything reminds you of an obligation or chore, remove it, store it, or toss it.

3. Add mood lighting.

Everyone looks better by lamplight than under an overhead

light. Consider placing lamps on the bedside tables and using no brighter than 60-watt bulbs. The key is creating a soft glow.

You may want to install a dimmer switch for the overhead light. There's a reason restaurants dim the lights in the evening. It creates ambiance and an atmosphere for romance.

Of course, candles are a must. Place several scented candles that welcome romance in various parts of the room. Remember, no clutter, so make sure the candles are actually a part of the décor and not an addition to a completed décor. I have a few small candles I keep in my nightstand to pull out when the time is right. Actually, Steve is usually the first one to pull out the candles!

Here's another idea when it comes to candles: Burn them. Too many women purchase and decorate with candles but don't burn them. So, girlfriend, burn those candles and heat up that bedroom.

4. Don't allow your room to be the kids' playroom.

I love children! However, when it comes to Mommy and Daddy's bedroom, the kids need to know that the bedroom is their special place. Don't allow it to become a second playroom for the kids with toys scattered about. Make sure the bedroom is a playroom for Mom and Dad.

5. Decorate with memories.

Frame pictures that remind you of special memories as husband and wife: your wedding day, a special romantic getaway, or an adventure you shared. You could also include a photo from your dating days to remind you of where it all began. One of my artsy friends used colored pencils to embellish our wedding invitation, placed it in a lovely frame, and gave it to us as a wedding gift. It has been in our bedroom through many moves for more than 36 years.

6. Remove the one-eyed monster.

I know I'm going to get some pushback on this one, but a television in the bedroom is a really bad idea. Sabrina Beasley McDonald wrote the following for FamilyLife.com:

> Spending time in front of the television keeps the attention off of your lives and onto shadows of life. Before you know it, your time together before bed slips away through the world of media. Bob DeMoss, author of *T.V.: The Great Escape*, wrote, "I am convinced that the simple decision to unplug TV [even] for just one month has the power to revolutionize our relationships with our spouse, our children, our world, and most importantly with our God." Just by the simple act of removing the TV, you open up free time to reconnect with your spouse in a special way without distractions.[2]

Dr. Paul Pearsall, author of *Super Marital Sex*, says:

> TV addiction is one of the most detrimental influences on American marriages. It is a shared addiction, which is the worst type, because it

sometimes covertly robs the relationship of available time for intimacy while both partners take
unknowing part in the theft.[3]

So take it out. If you want to lie down while you watch
television, do it on the couch or in a recliner. Save the bedroom for something better.

7. Make the bedroom a no-cell-phone zone.

We all know cell phones are a distraction...period. If there
is one place we don't want distraction, it's in the bedroom.
Can you imagine a husband hurrying through lovemaking
because he heard his phone ping with a new text message and
wants to know what it says? It happens! Can you imagine a
wife letting her mind wander away from loving her husband
because the phone rang and she now wonders who it was? It
happens! So make the bedroom a no-cell-phone zone. Set up
your charging station in another part of the house. For us it is
in the kitchen—out of sight and out of mind.

If you have to use your phone for your alarm clock...well,
you really don't. You can purchase an alarm clock for ten bucks.
But, if you feel like you have to use your phone for an alarm
clock, put it on "do not disturb" at a certain time, and it will
go silent until a time you set for the next day.

8. Fill the room with yummy scents and sounds.

Don't you just love refreshing scents? Make your room

an olfactory pleasure with candles, linen mists, or fragrant plug-ins. While you're at it, consider using one certain body mist that will leave the fragrance of you lingering on his mind. Memories are often linked with certain smells. Consider having one candle fragrance or pillow mist that will always remind your husband of your bedroom.

Play romantic music during times of intimacy or when you are simply in the bedroom relaxing.

9. Make the bedroom a no-work zone.

If anything in your bedroom can be found in an office, place it in another room. That includes printers, computers, and work desks. If you're cramped for space, consider setting up a workspace in a closet.

Avoid doing household chores in the bedroom. No ironing, no folding laundry, no paying bills. Nada.

10. Be *bedspirational.*

Perhaps you've invested in a great table for the breakfast room, a comfy sofa for the family room, and granite countertops for the kitchen. But what about your bed? Is it old? Ugly? Drab? Rickety? Perhaps you're still using the old hand-me-down from Mom and Dad. Part of making the bedroom the most important room in the house is to invest in a beautiful bed. But if that's not in your budget at this time, consider making your existing bed more appealing. A new duvet, pillow covers, and a throw can make all the difference.

And fluffy throw pillows make a beautiful splash. Stores like Bed Bath & Beyond have bed-in-a-bag sets with everything you need.

If you're on a tight budget, spend your money on a great box spring and mattress, but save on the headboard. Visit a thrift shop to find used headboards and footboards. With a fresh coat of paint, they can look amazing. Even better, use chalk paint to give the piece a romantic, up-to-date French country look. I've refurbished several pieces with homemade chalk paint. It's easy and beautiful. Check out Pinterest for ideas.

11. Invest in comfortable sheets.

Consider using silk or satin sheets for special occasions. If they're too pricey, 100 percent cotton sateen sheets also have a nice, cozy feel to them.

12. Wash your sheets often.

Nothing is more romantic than clean fresh smelling sheets! Use a fabric softener sheet for extra yumminess.

13. Add two comfortable chairs or a small love seat.

If you have room, add two comfortable upholstered chairs or a small love seat so that you and your husband can have quiet relaxing time to sit and share. You want to have some- where to sit other than the bed.

14. Share these ideas with your husband.

Tell your husband that you want your bedroom to be the

most romantic room in the house. Then share these ideas with him. You may want to ask him if he has any ideas of ways to make the bedroom more romantic. When he understands that you're trying to create an environment that is more conducive to passion, he'll probably jump in and help!

10 Easy Steps to Writing a Love Letter

Maybe you've never thought about writing a love letter and you're not quite sure where to start. I can assure you that if you give it a try, your husband will read your letter time and time again. I have an entire box of love letters my mother- and father-in-law wrote to each other during the two years he was in the Aleutian Islands in the Korean War. After they passed away, we found the letters tucked away in a closet. The letters were treasure they had kept for over 60 years of marriage, and now treasure we value as well.

So create some treasures of your own.

1. Begin by putting the date at the top of the letter. In the future, you will be glad you can see the date and remember when you wrote the words.

2. The most meaningful love letter is one written by hand, not typed out on a computer. There's just something about a handwritten note that's more personal and endearing.

3. Don't try too hard to make it sound like what you think a love letter should sound like. Write from your heart and don't try to sound like anyone else.

4. Think about what you would want your husband to know if these were the last words you were ever going to say to him. Let him know from the start why you are writing. "I am writing to let you know how much I love you." "I am writing because I have been thinking about how special our relationship is." "I am writing because I have been thinking about how much God has blessed me with you for a husband."

5. If you don't know where to start, consider using your past, present, and future as a general outline.

   Past: Write about the first time you met, what made you fall in love, when you knew he was the man you wanted to marry.

   Present: Write about what you love about him, the little things he does you cherish, his character, the way he looks in the morning, the way he thrills you still, how safe you feel when you're in his arms.

   Future: Write about how excited you are to spend the rest of your life with him, the anticipation you feel about making cherished memories, the

comfort you feel in knowing your love will
continue to grow with the passing years.

6. Make it specific by mentioning special memories
   or events only the two of you share.

7. Write words you think he would like to hear, not
   necessarily what you would want to hear.

8. Write a rough draft of your letter. Don't worry
   about grammar or spelling in the rough draft; just
   get your thoughts down on paper. Once you're
   satisfied with what you've written and proofed it
   for errors, copy it onto a clean sheet of paper.

9. End the letter with a meaningful closing such as
   "With all my heart," "Love forever," "Your adoring
   wife," or "Forever yours."

10. Make sure to sign your name.

Now that you've written your love letter, you might want
to consider making it a yearly ritual. Write letters for anniver-
saries, birthdays, or for no particular reason at all. Imagine
reading the letters in your golden years and seeing the dates
at the top of the pages. Even if you are already in your golden
years, it's not too late to start.

Notes

Day 1: Romance—It's Not Just for Us Girls

1. Willard Harley, *His Needs Her Needs: Building an Affair-Proof Marriage* (Grand Rapids, MI: Fleming H. Revell, 1986), 9.

2. Ibid., 10.

3. Harley 39.

4. Harley 41.

5. Alan Loy McGinnis, *The Romance Factor* (New York: HarperCollins, 1982) 198.

Day 2: Simple Surprises with Big Impact

1. Sheldon Vanauken, *A Severe Mercy* (New York: Bantam Books, 1977), 27.

Day 3: The Golden Keys of Admiration and Appreciation

1. Dr. Willard Harley, *His Needs, Her Needs* (Grand Rapids, MI: Fleming H. Revell, 1986), 151.

2. Ibid., 159.

3. Dr. Steve Stephens, *20 (Surprisingly Simple) Rules and Tools for a Great Marriage* (Carol Stream, IL: Tyndale, 2003), 17-19.

Day 4: Speaking Your Husband's Love Language

1. Gary Chapman, *The Five Love Languages*. To learn more about the five love languages, see Gary Chapman, *The Five Love Languages* (Chicago, IL: Northfield Publishing, 1992, 2004).

2. Stephen Covey, *The 7 Habits of Highly Effective People* (New York: Free Press, 1989), 238.

Day 5: Marveling at God's Divine Design

1. Linda Dillow and Lorraine Pintus, *Intimate Issues* (Colorado Springs: WaterBrook Press), 7.

Day 6: Making Marriage a Priority

1. Clifford and Joyce Penner, *The Gift of Sex* (Nashville: W Publishing Group, 2003), 197.

2. Lauren Boyer, "For a Happy Marriage, Have Sex This Many Times a Day," http://www.usnews.com/news/articles/2015/11/18/how-often-should-married-couples-have-sex.

3. Linda Carol, "To Be Happy Together, How Often Does a Couple Need Sex?" http://www.today.com/health/be-happy-together-how-often-does-couple-need-sex-t56561.

4. Kevin Leman, *Sheet Music: Uncovering the Secrets of Sexual Intimacy in Marriage* (Carol Stream, IL: Tyndale House Publishers, 2003), 46.

5. Ibid., 47.

Day 7: Keeping Hubby First

1. Sandra P. Aldrich, *Men Read Newspapers, Not Minds,* (Carol Stream, IL: Tyndale House Publishers), 145.

2. Rob Parsons, "Don't Let Your Baby Drive You Apart," *Focus on the Family,* February 1998, 12.

3. John Roseman, "Promise Keepers Challenges Husbands, but What About Wives?" *The Charlotte Observer,* February 10, 1998, 6E.

Day 8: Applying the Superglue of Marriage

1. Kevin Leman, *Sheet Music: Uncovering the Secrets of Sexual Intimacy in Marriage* (Carol Stream, IL: Tyndale House Publishing, Inc., 2003), 10.

2. Hank Ersch and Kostya Kennedy, "Scorecard," *Sports Illustrated,* August 17, 1998.

3. Leman, *Sheet Music,* 46.

4. Bill and Pam Farrel, *Red-Hot Monogamy* (Eugene, OR: Harvest House Publishers, 2006), 10-11.

5. Emerson Eggerichs, PhD, *Love & Respect* (Nashville: Thomas Nelson, 2004), 253.

Day 9: Recharging His Battery

1. John Gray, *Mars and Venus in the Bedroom* (New York: HarperCollins, 1995), 63.

2. Quoted in Jill Suttie and Jason Marsh, "5 Ways Giving Is Good for You," http://greatergood.berkeley.edu/article/item/5_ways_giving_is_good_for_you.

3. Ibid.

4. "Summer Love Science: How Exercise and Endorphins Impact Romance," http://www.keen.com/articles/love/summer-love-science-how-exercise-and-endorphins-impact-romance.

5. Ed Wheat, MD, and Gaye Wheat, *Intended for Pleasure* (Revell, 4th edition, 2010), 135.

Day 10: Letting Him Know You *Want* Him!

1. Meeting Your Husband's Romantic Needs http://www.familylife.com/articles/topics/marriage/staying-married/wives/meeting-your-husbands-romantic-needs.

2. "Meeting Your Husband's Romantic Needs," http://www.familylife.com/articles/topics/marriage/staying-married/wives/meeting-your-husbands-romantic-needs.

3. Sheila Wray Gregoire, Blog: *To Love, Honor, and Vacuum* http://tolovehonorand-vacuum.com/2010/12/wifey-wednesday-why-youve-got-to

Day 11: Remembering What You Need to Remember, Forgetting What You Need to Forget

1. Linda J. Waite and Maggie Gallagher, *The Case for Marriage* (New York: Doubleday, 2000), 148.

2. Judith Wallerstein, Julia M. Lewis, and Sandra Blakeslee, *The Unexpected Legacy of Divorce* (New York: Hyperion, 2000), 295.

3. C.S. Lewis, *The Weight of Glory* (New York: HarperCollins, 2001; originally published 1949), 181.

4. C.S. Lewis, *Mere Christianity* (Nashville: Broadman and Holman, 1996), 104.

5. Stormie Omartian, *The Power of a Praying Wife*, (Eugene, OR: Harvest House Publishers, 1997), 13.

6. Lewis Smedes, *Forgive and Forget* (San Francisco: Harper and Row, 1984), xxi, 146.

Day 12: Serving Love on a Silver Platter

1. Dennis Rainey, *Lonely Husbands, Lonely Wives* (renamed *Staying Close*) (Dallas: Word, 1989), 31.

Day 13: Creating an Atmosphere of Anticipation

1. Stephen Covey, *The 7 Habits of Highly Effective People* (New York: Simon and Schuster, 1989), 98-99.

2. Linda Dillow and Lorraine Pintus, *Intimate Issues* (Colorado Springs, CO: WaterBrook Press), 13.

Day 14: Responding to Him

1. Kevin Leman, *Sheet Music: Uncovering the Secrets of Sexual Intimacy in Marriage* (Carol Stream, IL: Tyndale House Publishing, Inc., 2003), 52.

2. Ibid. 11.

14 Tips for a More Romantic Bedroom

1. *Today News,* "Navy SEAL's Advice to Grads: Make Your Bed Every Morning," http://www.today.com/news/navy-seals-advice-grads-make-your-bed-every-morning-2D79695461.

2. Sabrina Beasley McDonald, "10 Ways to Create a More Romantic Bedroom,"

http://www.familylife.com/articles/topics/marriage/staying-married/romance-and-sex/10-ways-to-create-a-more-romantic-bedroom.

3. Dr. Paul Pearsall, *Super Marital Sex: Loving for Life* (New York: Doubleday Book Club, 1987), 16.

LET'S STAY CONNECTED

Now that we're friends, let's stay connected. One of the best ways is by signing up to receive my blog posts and email announcements. The *14-Day Romance Challenge* book is the result of 25,000 women who signed up to receive my 14-Day Romance Challenge through my blog posts back in 2013. This is just a sample of the many encouraging and helpful resources that will land in your email box each week for free. So sign up at www.sharonjaynes.com and let's stay in touch.

You can also find me on:

Facebook (www.facebook.com/sharonjaynes)

Twitter (www.twitter.com/sharonjaynes)

Instagram (www.instagram/sharonejaynes.com)
(note that little "e" between Sharon and Jaynes)

Pinterest (www.pinterest.com/sharonjaynes)

INVITE SHARON TO SPEAK
AT YOUR NEXT WOMEN'S EVENT

Sharon loves encouraging and equipping women to live fully and free in Christ. Her books are blessing women all around the world. But perhaps one of her greatest joys is speaking to women face-to-face at women's conferences, retreats, and events. If you would like to inquire about Sharon speaking at your next event, please visit her website at www.sharonjaynes.com!

OTHER MARRIAGE RESOURCES
BY SHARON JAYNES

Becoming the Woman of His Dreams

Praying for Your Husband from Head to Toe

Praying Wives App

The Praying Wives Facebook Page
(www.facebook.com/theprayingwivesclub)